KT-165-738

EX LIBRIS

CHERISHED LIBRARY

Gabriel N Cherish

WHISKY A Very Peculiar History™

A wee drop o' the hard stuff

'Come, let me know what it is
that makes a Scotchman happy!'
Dr Samuel Johnson (1709–1784)

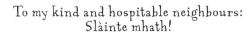

To my kind and hospitable neighbours:
Slàinte mhath!

FMacD

Editor: Stephen Haynes
Additional artwork: David Antram, Penko Gelev,
John James, Li Sidong, Mark Williams

Published in Great Britain in MMXI by
Book House, an imprint of
The Salariya Book Company Ltd
25 Marlborough Place, Brighton BN1 1UB
www.salariya.com
www.book-house.co.uk

HB ISBN-13: 978-1-907184-76-5

1 3 5 7 9 8 6 4 2
A CIP catalogue record for this book is available
from the British Library.
Printed and bound in Dubai.
Printed on paper from sustainable sources.

Visit our website at **www.book-house.co.uk**
or go to **www.salariya.com**
for **free** electronic versions of:
You Wouldn't Want to be an Egyptian Mummy!
You Wouldn't Want to be a Roman Gladiator!
You Wouldn't Want to be a Polar Explorer!
**You Wouldn't Want to sail on a 19th-Century
Whaling Ship!**

WHISKY
A Very Peculiar History™

A wee drop o' the hard stuff

Fiona Macdonald

Created and designed by
David Salariya

Illustrated by
Mark Bergin

Scotch drink

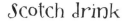

Scotland's favourite poet praises Scotland's favourite drinks, whisky and beer.

O thou, my Muse! Guid auld Scotch drink,
Whether through wimplin' worms thou jink,
Or, richly brown, ream o'er the brink,
   In glorious faem,
Inspire me, till I lisp and wink,
   To sing thy name!

          Robert Burns, 'Scotch Drink', 1786

Muse: source of inspiration
Guid auld: good old
wimplin': curling
worms: parts of distilling apparatus; cooled copper pipes in which
* vaporised alcohol condenses.*
jink: twist and turn
ream: flow
faem: foam
lisp: speak with difficulty.

Contents

INTRODUCTION

Scotland in a bottle?

'Whisky is a great industry in Scotland. Whisky is a great pleasure in the rest of the world.' So says French whisky writer Jean-Marie Putz. The statistics agree with him. In Scotland, around 10,000 people are employed full-time making and selling Scotch whisky, while a further 35,000 jobs are linked to the whisky trade. In 2007, whisky exports accounted for 13% of Scotland's overseas earnings, and contributed over £2.7 billion to Scotland's economy. Worldwide, over 300 million litres are sold – and presumably drunk with pleasure – every year.

A magic potion?

Whisky is only a solution of malt (grain sugar), yeast and water, but it has been praised and prized for hundreds of years. It is surrounded by countless legends and beliefs about its supposedly mystical, magical qualities. According to a 17th-century Scottish manuscript, whisky will (in this order):

- heal wounds
- polish brass
- sharpen the wits
- make a sad man happy
- preserve youth
- help women to conceive
- make good wine out of stale
- and much, much, much more.

Today, inexpensive, mass-produced whisky blends are widely available. They are piled high and sold cheap on supermarket shelves – although they are perhaps not yet cheap enough to use as metal polish. But fine whisky is still a rare and costly luxury; a single bottle can cost a small fortune.

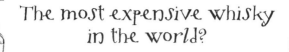

The most expensive whisky in the world?

In November 2010, international auction house Sotheby's in New York sold what was advertised as 'the world's most expensive bottle of whisky'. It was filled with highly prized 64-year-old malt whisky from Scotland's famous Macallan distillery.

The price? Estimates started at US$150,000, but the bottle actually fetched US$460,000 (GB £288,000).[1] But perhaps the most valuable part of this very, very costly item was the decanter it came in. Hand-crafted by Lalique of France in exquisite crystal, it was a unique work of art.

On the other hand, if you'd like to drink history, the last surviving bottle in the universe of Irish Nuns' Island whiskey also went on sale in 2010. The Nuns' Island distillery closed almost 100 years earlier. Who knows what the whiskey will taste like? You can find out if you have the asking price for such a unique rarity: £100,000.

1. The proceeds were donated to a charity that supplies clean drinking water to developing countries.

Tasting notes

The taste of whisky is easy to recognise but extremely difficult to describe. Unbelievable numbers – and combinations – of adjectives and nouns have been used to communicate its appearance, flavour and aroma, sometimes successfully:

- beautiful custard poured over barley pie

- bandages and antiseptic

- Parma violets, with some damp hay

- busy, sweaty sock

- a slight hint of liquorice/trout fishing basket

- wet cement

- freshly hung wallpaper

- celery and citrus

- pillow-soft vanilla

- a tang of gunpowder and a warm nuttiness.

In the case of one very memorable bottle:

- **It doesn't just hit the palate, it caresses it with the nubile fingers of a young lady and the talons of an eagle.**

Jim Murray's Whisky Bible 2010

One further fact for whisky connoisseurs to consider: different casks and bottlings of famous whiskies are known not as prosaic 'packaging', but as much more poetic 'expressions'. Do we wonder why?

Whisky's worldwide winners

The name of 'Scotch', together with its composition, packaging and promotion, is strictly protected and controlled – and yet local 'whiskies' are made and enjoyed all round the world, from Argentina to New Zealand. In 2010, a whisky made in India was chosen as third finest in the world, out of almost 4,000 different bottles! An American whiskey came first, and a Scottish whisky second. Indians now drink more whisky than any other nationality. They consumed 1,179 million litres in 2009 – and two thirds of this was produced in India.

Jekyll and Hyde?

Like the Scots themselves, and like the famous two-faced character invented by Scottish writer Robert Louis Stevenson (1850–1894),

Dr Jekyll

whisky is paradoxical. It takes great skill and many years to produce, but is often carelessly consumed in seconds. It wrecks budgets, ruins marriages, wastes lives – and yet few celebrations are complete without it. Nor are funerals. Traditionally, in Scotland, only men accompanied a body to the grave. Then, in even the most sober, upright families, it was an accepted sign of respect to drink 'the funeral dram'.

Mr Hyde

Why mince words?

*Notice outside a pub in a tough district
of Glasgow:*

WINES, BEERS & SPIRITS

• PUBLIC BAR •

FUNERALS CATERED FOR

None of your effete
southern 'function
rooms', eh?

Whisky or whiskey?

Both spellings are correct, although 'whisky' is normally used by distillers in Scotland, Canada, Japan, Australia, India, Brazil, Wales and elsewhere in Europe (except Ireland).

Scottish whisky is often also called 'Scotch' – but never in Scotland! There, it is called whisky, or, more hospitably, 'a dram'. Although a dram was originally a very small liquid measure used by pharmacists (one eighth of a fluid ounce, or about 3.7 ml – but definitions vary), today it refers to any quantity of whisky offered by a host to a guest, from a thimbleful to an overflowing tumbler.

And remember – in Scotland and Ireland, whisky is always 'taken', not drunk. As in: 'You'll take a wee dram, Hamish?'

The spelling 'whiskey' is said to have been invented by distillers in 19th-century Ireland, to distinguish their high-quality, traditionally made whisky from cheap, bland, 'industrial' whisky mass-produced in the Lowlands of Scotland (see Chapter 5). Today, 'whiskey' is commonly used by distillers in Ireland, New Zealand and the United States. However, a few American companies, mostly those founded by Scottish emigrants, prefer Scottish-style 'whisky'.

Wearable whisky?

In 2007, whisky enthusiast Edgar van der Crommert, from the Netherlands, designed a new tartan in honour of Scottish malt whisky. He chose colours and patterns carefully to 'tell the whisky story'. Each element in the design symbolises either a whisky ingredient, or a stage in the manufacturing process:

1. Yellow lines: ripe barley

2. Brown squares: ploughed fields

3. Black squares: peat

4. Light brown lines: yeast

5. Dark blue squares: spring water

6. Pale blue lines: distilled spirit

7. Brown lines: barrels

8. Black lines: bonded warehouse

9. Faint blue lines: 'the angels' share' (evaporating spirit; see page 137)

10. White lines: glass bottles

11. Wide yellow stripe: the end product.

The very devil...

Whisky is glamorous and seductive. It plays a strong supporting role in classic Hollywood films of the 1940s and 1950s, and in stylish US detective stories written by the likes of Dashiell Hammett and Raymond Chandler. It's drunk by gumshoes, gangsters – and their molls. Like them, it's smart and stylish.

Whisky is sordid and repulsive. It features in many gritty novels of despair and self-destruction, mostly by Scottish authors. These range from the deliberately dour *House with Green Shutters* (George Douglas Brown, 1901 – the hero gets drunk and murders) to the defiant *No Mean City* (H. Kingsley Long and Alexander McArthur, 1935 – the hero gets drunk and is murdered) and the tough, tragic *Morvern Callar* (Alan Warner, 1995 – where the heroes – or victims – mainline on Macallan and much else besides).

'Whisky, no doubt, is a devil, but why has this devil so many worshippers?'

Scottish judge Lord Cockburn (1799–1854)

16

Whisky drowns sorrows. It inspires songs and poems. It sustains heroes, wins worldwide fans, has its own tartan – and is a gift to the Scottish tourist trade. Above all, it is convivial:

> 'Here's a bottle and an honest friend.
> What wad ye wish for mair, Man?'[2]

> *Robert Burns – who else?*

So, just exactly what is this magical – or malignant – Scottish liquid treasure? When (and where) did it originate?

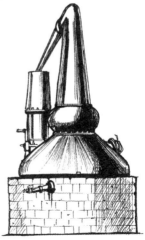

This modern industrial still works on exactly the same principle as the ancient one on page 26.

2. *wad: would; mair: more.*

THE WATER OF LIFE

Today's name 'whisky' comes from two Scottish Gaelic words, *uisge beatha* (say: OOSH-kee-baw), meaning 'water of life'. However, several other liquids have carried similar names, at different times and in different places. Or else they've been given nicknames: either euphemistic (as in vodka, which means 'little water' or 'just a drop!'), or else describing their place of origin, their ingredients, or even (as in the case of rum) their effects on the drinker.

Some 'strong waters' of the world

Name	Meaning	Origin	Made from
Aqua vitae	water of life	medieval Europe	grapes
Eau de vie (brandy)	"	France	grapes
Akavit		Scandinavia	grain
Vodka	little water	Russia	grain, bread, (later) potatoes
Grappa	grapes	Italy	grape skins
Rum	uproar	Caribbean	sugar cane
Arak	strong water or sweat	Middle East	grapes
Arrack	"	Southeast Asia	fruit, sugar cane, coconut sap
Moonshine	made at night	North America	grain
Poitin (potcheen)	little pot	Ireland	grain
Tequila	city where first made	Mexico	agave cactus

Distillation

Apart from their weird and wonderful names, what else do these 'waters of life' have in common? They are all strong alcoholic drinks, produced by *distillation*.

Distillation is a basic physical process. You simply:

- **heat a liquid until it boils**
- **capture the resulting hot vapours and cool them so that they condense**
- **then collect the condensed liquid.**

Today, scientists use distillation as an important analytical tool. The different components of any organic compound boil at different temperatures; distilling isolates them so that they can be identified.

Distillation is also used to purify all kinds of compounds. Water and other unwanted elements can be vaporised (turned to steam), collected and disposed of, leaving only a pure concentrate behind.

Perfume and paint

Distillation has a very ancient history. It was probably invented in the Middle East and used for making perfumes. Pottery jars with rims designed to catch drops of cooled vapour have survived from around 3500 BC. Much later, around 400 BC, ancient Greek scientists distilled metallic salts, hoping to create longer-lasting pigments for artists. By around AD 1150, in Muslim Spain and multicultural Sicily, experimenters had perfected techniques for distilling alcohol to make and preserve medicines.

But not to drink?

In the past, the Islamic tradition of abstaining from alcoholic drinks was less well observed in some Muslim civilisations than in others. But all Muslim doctors warned of alcohol's dangerous effects. Central Asian scholar Ibn Sina (c.980–1037; known in the West as Avicenna), the greatest scientific genius of his age, is said to have cautioned:

'To give wine to youths is like putting fire on top of fire.'

Skill or sorcery?

Ibn Sina was a careful, observant philosopher and physician. However, to many people of his time, the process of distillation seemed mysterious and magical – part of alchemy, not science. It was a secret skill, belonging only to a few rather sinister scholars. These learned men (and some women) had the education (they could read and write), the training (they studied with older, wiser masters) and the money (usually from rich patrons) to set up laboratories and buy books, rare ingredients and elaborate equipment.

Unlike scientific or medical distillers, who had practical purposes for their investigations, alchemists were engaged in an esoteric quest. They aimed to transform the raw material of this world into a higher state, by separating 'base' (low) elements[1] from purer, more 'spiritual' ones. If each substance could be refined by distilling over and over again, then only its pure 'quintessence' would remain.

1. From ancient Greek times until around 1700, many people believed that the world was made of four elements: earth (the lowest, most base), air, fire and water. All these were changeable: they decayed and died.

It would become ethereal,[2] like the stars. As an added attraction, the same process would also – according to alchemists' theories – turn base metals into gold.

Bubble, bubble...

To dissolve base substances and hopefully transform them, medieval alchemists pioneered and improved distilling technology. They lit fierce wood fires under metal cauldrons, filled the cauldrons with the substance to be distilled, set it to boil, and collected the vapours that arose in vessels called alembics, retorts and pelicans.

2. There was also thought to be a fifth element, ether. It was what the heavens were made of, and was not normally present on earth. It was incorruptible: it lasted for ever.

Pelicans?

No, not the big-beaked bird but a strange-shaped glass vessel. This had a pair of long, narrow, tapering arms bent over like jug handles. The shape reminded medieval people of holy pictures showing mother pelicans stabbing their breasts with their beaks, then feeding their chicks with the blood. (Christian preachers taught that pelicans were a symbol of Jesus, who shed his own blood to save sinners.)

The long neck of the alchemists' *retort* had a rather different purpose. When the liquid in the vessel was set to boil over a cauldron, the vapours cooled at the top of the neck, and the distilled liquid then ran down into another container in a slow, controllable way. *Fractional distillation* (collecting separate, measured portions of the distilled liquid, each containing different substances) was invented in Salerno, Sicily, around AD 1250.

Retort

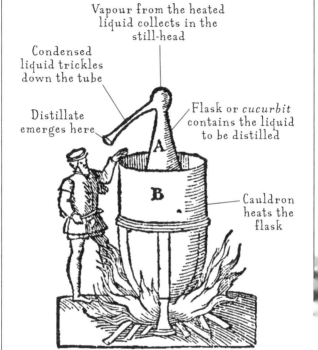

Vapour from the heated liquid collects in the still-head

Condensed liquid trickles down the tube

Distillate emerges here

Flask or *cucurbit* contains the liquid to be distilled

A

B

Cauldron heats the flask

A 16th-century alchemist's still

The still-head and tube together are called the *alembic*; but this term may also be used to refer to the whole apparatus. When the flask and the alembic are made in one piece, they form a *retort*.

Everlasting

Usually, distillation was repeated many times – the more vigorous (and dangerous) the boiling, the better! The side-arms of the pelican led the condensed vapours back into the vessel to be distilled again. As 16th-century German doctor and alchemist, Conrad Gesner, explained:

'The distilled...substance...contains in itself the four elements, but due to the continuous motion and agitation, it is converted from corruptible into incorruptible.'

Scientifically speaking, this is not true. But, compared with grapes or grain or sugar cane, or any other of the raw materials from which waters of life were made, distilled liquids did seem to have the magical ability never to rot or go bad, but to survive for ever.

Would drinkers of distilled waters of life absorb some of this supernatural power? No-one could be sure, but it was worth a try.

To Scotland - how and why?

It's a long way from Arabia and Greece to Scotland, even today. How – and when – did knowledge of the ancient invention of distillation make the journey? No-one knows for certain, but there are three possibilities:

• **Soldiers and science**
Muslim scholars such as Ibn Sina studied ancient Greek scientific texts, combining their contents with ideas from India, Persia and Arab lands. As Muslim armies marched westwards into Europe, Muslim scientific knowledge spread with them.

• **Rich and rare**
Kings and chiefs in Ireland and southwest Scotland loved expensive, exotic luxuries. From around AD 500 they imported wine, spices, silks, medicines and fine swords from traders in southern Europe and the Middle East. Slowly, knowledge of new technologies, including distilling, also spread northwards.

• Wandering monks

Scottish – and Irish – monks were great travellers. Although some, like Ireland's St Columbanus (died AD 615), were famous for destroying drink,[3] others went to study at top European universities. There, from around AD 1200, they learned how to make and use distilled medicines, and brought the knowledge back home with them.

All – or none – of these possibilities might be true. But what we do know is that the first definite reference to 'water of life' in Scotland comes from the late 15th century AD. What, precisely, does it say?

3. Columbanus blasted a cauldron of beer being used for a pagan festival. The Celts had been skilful brewers since Roman times. Columbanus also won fame for giving orders to a fierce wild bear; it obeyed him.

CHAPTER TWO

MONKS, MEDICINE AND MAGIC

The first reference to whisky production in Scotland comes from Scottish exchequer rolls (tax records) dated 1494. In that year, on the orders of King James IV of Scotland, royal officials gave 'eight bolls[1] of malt to Brother John Cor wherewith to make aqua vitae'.

That was enough malt to make between 1,250 and 1,500 modern bottles of whisky. So Brother John was presumably not a novice experimenter. He belonged to the rich and

1. *about 1,692 litres or 870 kg.*

prestigious Benedictine abbey at Lindores in Fife, where there was a long tradition of learning. And King James's royal bulk order suggests that whisky production – and consumption – were well established in Scotland by the late 15th century.

first make your beer...

Sadly, Brother John's recipe for whisky has not survived. But it's likely to have been very simple, and based on Scottish tradition. Whisky is basically distilled ale or beer, and Celtic peoples had been famous for their skill as beer-makers since ancient Roman times. They made beer by:

- mashing (boiling) malted grain in a large quantity of water

- straining out the grains

- re-boiling the liquid (now called 'wort'), together with flavourings if required

- adding yeast (or letting wild, airborne yeasts settle on the wort), then letting the mixture ferment (bubble) until all the yeast had died.

Right royal drinker

King James IV (ruled 1488–1513) was one of Scotland's most popular rulers. Keenly interested in science, medicine, architecture, literature and art, he spoke six languages, experimented with making cannon – and with amateur dentistry – and commissioned Europe's most modern warships for the Scottish navy. He loved hunting and sport, and had many mistresses.

King James was also famous for being friendly and hospitable. He liked to wander in disguise round the mean streets of Stirling, chatting to ordinary people. And he built splendid new great halls in his castles, where he entertained his friends with music, feasting, dancing – and whisky.

It is just possible that the phrase 'a round of drinks' originated with royal party-givers like James. As a sign of friendship and esteem, he shared drinks with all the guests sitting around his table. They either passed a brimming goblet round the table from one drinker to another (a very ancient custom), or, more likely by King James's time, filled their cups and downed their drinks all together.

Favourite flavourings for early Scottish beer – and whisky – were taken from plants that grew locally, such as thyme, mint, fennel, juniper and cranberries. It was claimed that water from different sources also added its own special taste to each brew. Lindores Abbey had two well-known water supplies, the Monks' Well and the Abbot's Well. We do not know whether Brother John used these – or water from the nearby River Tay – in his distillations.

...then boil it

To make whisky, experts such as Brother John took freshly brewed beer (known as 'wash' to whisky professionals) and distilled it by boiling. This separated the alcohol from the water in the wash; the alcohol vaporised at a much lower temperature. As the wash was heated, the alcohol rose into the retort or alembic (long-beaked vessel), leaving the water behind.

Brother John's distilling equipment was probably similar to that used by medieval alchemists (see page 26), but on a much larger scale than most. Probably, the spout of his retort passed through a tub of water, to cool the distilled vapour inside it. This was a new, and very effective, 15th-century invention. Probably, too, Brother John distilled his whisky twice. That made a smoother, better-balanced brew. He may also have added a second batch of flavourings or medicinal herbs.

Distillers' skills

Why did King James favour Brother John with such a large order? Almost certainly because of his skill, taste and judgement. All these were needed to produce whisky that tasted good – and was safe to drink.

The alcoholic vapours that rise from a boiling tub of mash are not all the same, and are not all suitable for consumption. A good distiller has to know how to separate the 'heart' (middle fraction) of each distillation (which tastes good) from the unpleasant and sometimes harmful first and last fractions.

At your peril

Martin Martin (d. 1719), a Gaelic-speaking writer from the Isle of Skye, recorded that three different kinds of whisky were made in the Western Isles:

- **common usquebaugh**: distilled twice

- **trestarig**: distilled three times

- **usquebaugh-baul**: distilled four times – its Gaelic name means (with good reason) 'perilous whisky'.

'Two spoonfuls of this last liquor is a sufficient dose; and if any man exceed this, it would presently stop his breath…'

Martin Martin, A Description of the Western Islands of Scotland, *1703*

In 2010, a whisky company on the island of Islay released an experimental batch of 'perilous whisky'. It was phenomenally strong, containing 90% alcohol, compared with 40% in ordinary whisky – and was used in a TV stunt to power a high-performance sports car. Even though water was added to reduce the alcohol to 63.5% before the 'perilous whisky' was bottled, the producers were still condemned as 'irresponsible' by the Scotch Whisky Association.

First to distil and trickle down the spout of Brother John's alembic would have been the 'heads' or 'foreshots'. These are very strong, light, impure alcohols that taste unbearably pungent and bitter. Brother John would have put these aside, and waited until the drinkable 'heart' of the distilled vapour began running. That would have been sweetly scented with esters – natural chemicals that smell of fruit and flowers. After a while, Brother John's sensitive nose would have detected new, most unpleasant odours, such as sweat, rotten eggs or vomit. These marked the arrival of the 'feints' or 'aftershots': heavy, harsh, oily compounds in the last fraction of distilled liquid. The tiniest trace of them added 'body' to a whisky, but too much was disastrous.

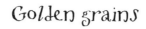

Golden grains

As King James's gift makes clear, Brother John did not make his own malt for distilling. That was a task for workers with different skills. Malt was – and still is – made by soaking grains in water, keeping them warm, allowing them to germinate and grow shoots, then drying them over heat, and, sometimes, smoking them. The heat ends the germination and kills the shoots, but not before enzymes (natural catalysts in each grain) have converted its starch into sugar. When dissolved in water, the sugary malt 'feeds' yeasts, which multiply and give off alcohol, ready for distilling.

Barley is the best grain for malting, because it is rich in enzymes, but when it was not available, Scottish maltsters used oats instead.

Bere, or two-row barley

Home is where the still is

By James IV's time, whisky was also being
made in small quantities by poor, ordinary
people. They may have learned to improve
their distilling techniques after monks were
forced to leave their monasteries in the mid-
16th century.[2] But most poor whisky-makers
used the very simplest of equipment – just a
pot with a spout heated over an open fire, and
a bowl or jug to catch the distilled liquid. As
late as 1904, Scottish Highlanders in remote
villages were said to make home-brew using
only 'the help of the kettle'.

A simple cottage
still, with a close-up
of a distilling vessel
in the foreground

A: base of flask
B: still-head
C: barrel of cold
    water to cool the
    pipe or 'worm'
D: pipe or 'worm'
E: alembic set over
    furnace

2. They were forced out by religious reformers. Brother John's
monastery at Lindores was destroyed by followers of Protestant preacher
John Knox in 1559.

The peat reek

Peat is a mass of partially decayed organic material. It makes bogs, and is made by them. It is formed when dead or dying plants, plus the remains of insects and small animals,[3] are prevented from rotting at their normal rate by acidic, airless surroundings – usually when they become completely covered by water. Over the centuries – many Scottish and Irish bogs are around 9,000 years old – the lower layers of dead material very slowly decay. They are also compressed by the weight of fresh dead plants above them, forming a sticky, solid black mass. If left undisturbed for millennia, this eventually turns into coal.

Until recently, peat was dug for fuel in Scotland, Ireland, Russia and many other boggy places. It was sliced into brick-sized slabs, left to dry all summer, then burnt in wintertime on an open fire. Traditionally, it was the fuel used to dry the sprouted grains used to make malt for Scottish distillers

3. not to mention the occasional human, such as the preserved body known as Lindow Man, who either fell in or, more likely, was sacrificed to Celtic gods.

(see page 38). Since peat smoulders rather than burns with a bright flame, its smoke passed on a distinctive flavour – the 'peat reek' – to the whisky.[4]

A warm welcome

As well as drinking for pleasure, Scottish people used whisky as a restorative, or even as a medicine. Swallowing it produced an instant glow of apparent wellbeing; as the Scots said, 'it kept out the cold'. A wee dram also warmed and welcomed travellers arriving at isolated Highland farms after long walks or rides in bad weather. In the mid-19th century a Scottish noblewoman recalled how a barefoot Highland woman, with two young children at her side, arrived at the local 'big house' with a message. As was the custom, she was thanked and given a cup of whisky. When the woman offered a sip to each of the children, the lady of the big house was horrified. She asked the older child, 'Doesn't it bite you?' The child replied, 'Ay, but I like the bite.'

4. Reek *is a Scots word for 'smoke'.*

The bride's cog

Strengthening drinks of whisky mixed with other rich ingredients were often drunk by couples on the night before their wedding, or by mothers about to give birth. In Orkney, this brew was prepared in a wooden tub (*coggan* in Gaelic). It contained ale, pepper, ginger, nutmeg, beaten eggs, toasted cake – and, of course, whisky.

Medicinal whisky

'May the Good Lord preserve us from the disease that whisky cannot cure.'

Traditional Highland saying

Don't try this at home!

This traditional Scottish treatment for diarrhoea sounds rather alarming:

1. Set fire to a cupful of whisky.

2. Let it burn for two or three minutes.

3. Put out the flames and drink it straight away.

That's better!

Whisky was one of the only 'medicines' available to most ordinary Scottish people. They were either too poor to pay for medical treatment, and/or had no doctor living within their community. It was specially recommended for 'trembling limbs' (presumably it had a sedative effect), for gum, tooth and throat disease (the alcohol may have acted as an antiseptic mouthwash), and as a cure for stomach cramps or colic (it may have relaxed tense muscles). When mixed with powdered sulphur, it was said to cure measles, which killed many young children in Scotland up until the late 19th century.

Herbs and spices

Burning whisky (as in the remedy described opposite) would have destroyed most of the alcohol that it contained. And, since whisky as medicine was often taken only in small quantities, or blended with milk or oatmeal, people did not rely solely on its alcoholic content when hoping for a cure. Possibly, the herbs and spices that were sometimes used to flavour it may have had some medicinal effect. A 'very old' recipe for Highland bitters (traditionally taken to aid the digestion) was recorded by pioneer Scottish food historian F. Marian McNeill (1885–1973). It included cloves, cinnamon, coriander, orange peel, gentian root and camomile flowers, all steeped – of course – in whisky.

Surgery – and spells

In Edinburgh, whisky was sold by barber-surgeons. Another early royal record, made by Scotland's Lord Treasurer, no less, accounts for money paid in 1498 to the 'barbour that brocht aqua vitae to the King [James IV again] in Dundee'. As well as cutting hair and shaving beards, barbers worked as junior doctors, letting blood (a popular cure for many ailments), sewing up cuts and performing dangerous, very painful surgery. Barbers probably used whisky as an anaesthetic, maybe for bathing infected wounds, and perhaps just to make their patients feel a little bit better.

Without access to barbers, ordinary people used whisky in health-giving and healing rituals, mingled with Christian prayers and/or pagan magic spells.

Horse sense?

Whisky was sometimes mixed with the feed given to horses, to revive them after great efforts. Or it was massaged into their legs to ease strains and sprains. (Scottish people rubbed whisky on their own injuries, too – and on their foreheads, to drive headaches away.) These 'whisky cures' for horses led to many taunting jokes between the Scots and the Irish, who were famous for their skill at horse-breeding, handling and training. The Scots said that Irish whiskey had originally been invented as horse liniment, and that Irish distillers had never bothered to improve it.

It's the only thing that keeps me going.

Good health and long life!

This ancient ritual to protect and name a new baby was reported surprisingly recently – in 1904:

1. Pour three glasses of whisky and three of wine into a tub of water. Add three spoonfuls of salt.

2. Place the tub on the hearth.

3. Dip three short swords into the tub.

4. Stand in a circle round the tub.

5. Pass the baby round the circle.

6. Wash the baby in the tub.

7. Give the baby a name and ask God to bless and protect it.

8. Give the baby a sip of milk mixed with whisky and honey.

9. Send whisky and oatcakes to family, friends and neighbours so they may drink the baby's health.

'A soveraigne liquour'

A 16th-century Englishman praises the medicinal benefits of aqua vitae:

'It slows age, it strengthens youth, it helps digestion, it cuts phlegm, it abandons melancholy, it relieves the heart, it lightens the mind, it quickens the spirits, it...pounces [powders] the [kidney] stone, it expels gravel [from urine], it puffs away all ventosity [wind], it keeps and preserves the head from whirling, the eyes from dazzling, the tongue from lisping,...the teeth from chattering, the throat from rattling, the weasan [gullet] from stifling, the stomach from wambling [feeling unsettled], the heart from swelling, the belly from retching, the guts from rumbling, the hands from shivering, the sinews from shrinking, the veins from crumpling, the bones from aching, the [bone] marrow from soaking... And truly it is a sovereign liquor, if it be orderly taken.'

Adapted from Raphael Holinshed, The Chronicles of England, Scotland and Ireland, *1577*

As the publishers of the revised (1587) edition of Holinshed's *Chronicles* remarked, they contain 'manifold matters of singular note and worthie memorie'.

Scotch – or what?

But what's this? Holinshed places his praise of strong spirits not in his text about Scotland, but in his volume on Ireland! And, although he mentions that Scottish people sometimes drink aqua vitae, it is obviously Ireland that is linked most closely with whisky in his mind. Jings! Or, maybe, Begorrah! Is Scotland's national drink not Scottish after all?

No-one really knows. Certainly, the first reference to distilling in Ireland dates to the 12th century: around 1170, English soldiers reported seeing monastic distilleries there. That is over 300 years before James IV sent malt to Brother John Cor. Traditional stories tell how early Christian dignitaries from France brought knowledge of distillation to Ireland around AD 431.

It is possible that Irish monks were the first in the British Isles to learn how to make aqua vitae, and later passed their knowledge on to their brothers in Scotland. Certainly, the Scots must have been eager to know. The demand for medicinal distilled liquors increased rapidly after the 1340s, when epidemic disease (including the Black Death) swept through Europe.

It is equally possible that Scottish monks and friars learned the art by travelling to Europe – or by welcoming European visitors – at about the same time as the Irish were learning their distillery skills. In central Europe we hear of invading Huns distilling a liquid made from barley as early as AD 448. And monks in Germany were distilling wine to make brandy, or 'burnt wine', by around 1150.

One final fact may reassure Scottish readers. Holinshed's text suggests that the Irish drank aqua vitae mainly for medicinal reasons. Their damp climate and boggy landscape made them 'subject to distillations, reumes and flires' – all kinds of nasty coughs, colds and chesty diseases. Unlike good King James and his friends, they were not drinking whisky for fun!

But, medicinal or not, early whisky probably killed quite a few people too. Its manufacture was unregulated and unlicensed, and the alcohol content was entirely uncontrolled…

Mouth and throat: cancer

Brain: impaired memory, blurred vision, hallucination, sleep disorders

Blood: anaemia

Stomach: gastritis

Heart: heart failure

Liver: cirrhosis, hepatitis

Pancreas: pancreatitis

The demon Drink

Heavy consumption of alcohol can damage many parts of the body.

CHAPTER THREE

WHAT'S YOUR POISON?

hisky is just one of many familiar, everyday substances that can change, enhance – and sometimes destroy – our lives. It's not whisky itself that's so powerful. Rather, it's the ethanol, also called ethyl alcohol, that it contains. Ethanol is also found in many other popular beverages, from beer and wine to vodka and brandy.

Ethanol belongs to a whole family of closely related chemicals – the alcohols. They include methanol (methyl or wood alcohol), used as a solvent in industry; and glycol, used in vehicle engines as an antifreeze. Alcohols are also used as antiseptics and disinfectants, and are ingredients in paints and cleaning products, in toiletries, perfumes and flavourings.[1] Alcohols have been burned to give heat and light. There are even alcohol-powered cars.

Most alcohols are extremely poisonous. Just one gulp of methanol can kill you. Strangely, ethanol is an antidote to many other kinds of alcohol poisoning – but never, never, never try to prove that at home.

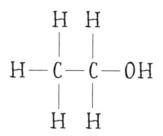

The chemical formula for ethanol is:
$$CH_3CH_2OH \text{ or } C_2H_5OH$$

1. For example, menthol – peppermint oil – is a natural alcohol from (yes) mint plants.

Losing control

Like other recreational drugs, ethanol can be very dangerous. It's seductive, it's addictive. It can make you feel good. Drinking with friends can be fun. But too much ethanol leads to loss of self control, and even to social disruption. It makes people talk long and loud, and lose their inhibitions. (Often they regret it the day after.) It makes them argue and fight, or take stupid risks. (They regret that, too.) It makes driving or handling machinery doubly dangerous. In the USA, over half of all deaths in motor accidents are due to drunken drivers.

Express delivery

A double whisky (50 ml) at standard strength (40% alcohol by volume) contains 110 kilocalories – and 16 g of pure ethanol.

The alcohol reaches the blood and the brain in just a few minutes, but can take at least two hours to be metabolised by the body, and still longer to leave it completely.

Good, bad or ugly?

Ethanol is also toxic. It's been blamed for causing depression, nausea, vomiting, clumsiness, blurred vision and impaired understanding. It cuts off the blood supply to our brains. It irritates the stomach and the skin. It damages the liver. It causes cancers, obesity – and accidents. It can even maim unborn babies.

However, in very small doses, our bodies can usually cope with it. And, while doctors do not all agree, some say that an occasional alcoholic drink (ideally whisky or red wine)[2] might even be good for us. It might, just might, help protect against some kinds of heart disease, strokes and cataracts.

2. *These contain natural anti-oxidant chemicals that help prevent damage to body cells.*

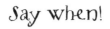

Say when!

'One glass: neither better nor worse.
Two glasses: the better, not the worse.
Three glasses: the worse, not the better.'

*Traditional Scottish saying about
drinking whisky*

Quite a glassful

We do not drink pure ethanol; even a strong 'spirit' drink such as whisky contains some water, together with acids, esters (see page 37), caramel (burnt sugar), tiny traces of powerful alcohols known as 'fusel oils', and buttery, winy, leathery or vanilla-like flavours absorbed from the wooden casks that the whisky has been stored in.

Since the 18th century, the alcoholic strength of liquors, including whisky, has been measured as 'proof'.

Proof of what?

When used to describe whisky and other high-alcohol drinks, 'proof' has nothing to do with criminals and law courts; it dates back to the time when suspicious sailors of the British Royal Navy wanted to be sure that their daily ration of rum had not been watered down and weakened. They knew that strong alcoholic drinks had the power to ignite gunpowder.[3] So new deliveries of rum to Royal Navy dockyards were 'proved' (tested)[4] to check that the distillers had supplied it at full strength. If the rum passed the test, it was declared to be '100 proof'.

Amazingly, the same definition of 'proof spirit' remained in use in the UK until 1980. After that, European Community law demanded that the strength of spirits sold in the UK should be shown on bottle labels as the percentage of alcohol (ethanol) by volume.

3. *Gunpowder catches fire when it is mixed with liquid containing a minimum of 57.15% alcohol by volume.*
4. *Nowadays this is done with a hydrometer rather than the more exciting but risky gunpowder method.*

However, in the wonderful world of whisky, things are very rarely simple and sometimes rather confusing. Today, alcoholic drinks like whisky are occasionally still labelled in 'degrees proof', as well as with the legal formula. This figure is usually expressed as a percentage, such as '50 degrees proof spirit'. But whisky buyers – and drinkers – beware! That is most definitely *not* the same as '50 per cent alcohol by volume'. Instead, it refers to the old naval standard of 'proof spirit'.[5]

By that measure, a bottle of 100% ethanol alcohol would be an amazing 175% proof. (It would also be undrinkable by anyone who wanted to survive!) A drink containing 50% alcohol by volume would be 87.5% proof; 'everyday' blended whisky,[6] which normally contains around 40% alcohol by volume, would be (40 x 1.75 = 70) degrees proof.

5. In which 57.15% alcohol by volume equalled 100% proof.
6. What my late lamented father used to call 'cooking whisky'.

America, America

Across the Atlantic, however, they do things rather differently. In the USA, alcoholic proof is defined as 'twice the percentage of alcohol by volume'. So bottles destined for the American market must have their own special labels. These will show, for example, that a whisky containing 50% alcohol by volume is 100-proof. (In the USA, the percentage sign is omitted.) Everyday whisky will be labelled '80-proof'.

In other words, the same whisky, in different markets, can appear to be significantly weaker or stronger, while staying just the same. Does this matter? Not to drinkers, probably – but it's important to the taxman (see Chapter 4).

'You have been warned!

'A sup of good whiskey will make you glad;
Too much of the Creature will set you mad;
If you take it in reason, 'twill make you wise;
If you drink to excess, it will close up
    your eyes...'

Irish traditional song, published in
The Universal Songster, 1826

fatal draught –
or the cup that kills

The old song is correct: too much whisky can
kill. Doctors and scientists reckon that 0.3%
alcohol by volume in the blood – from whisky
or anywhere else – is enough to cause
unconsciousness. At 0.4% there is a real risk of
fatality. At 0.55% or over you will very
probably be dead.

Indeed, one of the very first references to Irish
whiskey survives from 1405, when the Annals
of Clonmacnoise record the death of a

chieftain from 'a surfeit of aqua vitae'. And here is what happened on the Scottish whisky-making island of Islay in 1859:

In the springtime of the year, the brig (sailing ship) *Mary Ann* set off from Greenock on the River Clyde for New Brunswick in Canada. As she battled her way through stormy high seas, she hit rocks and was wrecked in Islay's Kilchoman Bay. Huge waves smashed her timbers and began to wash her cargo overboard. And what was in her hold? Yes, you've guessed – whisky, and lots of it (and some pig iron, too, for good measure). Around 2,400 bottles of gin, brandy and whisky reached Kilchoman beach, together with 'upwards of six' big barrels of whisky and wine.

Islay crofters and fishermen hurried to the shore. They grabbed, and quaffed, as many bottles as they could. As the *Greenock Advertiser* reported, with stern disapproval, 'the wildest scenes of drunkenness and riot' soon followed.

Worse was to come. Before long, the beach was littered with groaning, gasping drinkers, semi-conscious and unable to move among the

The brig *Mary Ann* gives new meaning to the phrase 'Scotch on the rocks'

rocks where they had collapsed. Others, according to the *Advertiser*, were 'fighting like savages'.

The end of the story is tragic. The strongest man on Islay, one Donald MacPhadyen, died of alcohol poisoning (he had in fact drunk more brandy than whisky). Many more were found 'apparently in a dying state'. At least two followed Donald to the grave; the rest eventually recovered.

On the other hand...

Whisky can also be extremely alluring. It makes positive appeal to all of the senses. Its bright golden glow pleases the eyes; its rich, complex smell intrigues the nose; its multi-layered taste, alcoholic 'nip' and smooth but substantial 'mouth feel' can all be very satisfying. Even hearing the 'glug' of whisky poured from a bottle into a glass calls up powerful responses, both physical (making the saliva flow) and psychological (cheering, comforting or exciting).

Shared pleasures

In 1775, famous English writer Dr Samuel Johnson went on a tour of mainland Scotland and the Western Isles with his Scottish friend James Boswell. 'Everywhere', Johnson remembered, 'we were treated like princes in our progress.'

Boswell also published an account of their travels, in 1785. In it he described Johnson examining Highland dress, swinging a massive claymore (Highland broadsword) above his head, listening to the bagpipes, and drinking whisky – though not all at the same time...

The friends were staying at Inverary, a small town in the west of Scotland, where:

'We supped well; and after supper, Dr. Johnson, whom I had not seen taste any fermented liquor during all our travels, called for a gill [142 ml] of whisky.

'"Come," (said he); "Let me know what it is that makes a Scotchman happy!"

'He drank it all but a drop, which I begged him leave to pour into a glass that I might say we had drunk whisky together.'

More and more

In spite of the risks and because of the pleasures, whisky drinking – and production – continued. And, although a Scottish law of 1597 tried to limit whisky distilling to 'earls, lords, barons or gentlemen…for their own use', it was mostly made by poor Scottish crofters (smallholders). They drank some themselves or shared it with neighbours, but a large amount was handed over to their landlords as rent. This arrangement ensured that the Scottish upper classes always had a plentiful supply of whisky to offer to their guests, and – if travellers' reports are to be believed – to drink themselves, at breakfast.

Something special

Johnson and Boswell stayed with many rich, grand people on their travels. And they were honoured guests; their generous hosts were keen to impress them with the very best of Scottish produce – and could afford to drink whisky whenever they chose. But for most ordinary Scottish people whisky remained a drink for extraordinary occasions. The 'water of life' was sipped to mark the crucial turning-points of human existence, from welcoming a newborn baby in its cradle to bidding farewell to a dead body in its grave. On such occasions, whisky's perilous, quasi-magical powers seemed entirely appropriate. Whisky also offered the hope of healing, sometimes when all else had failed.

Awaiting the morning dram

'They are not a drunken race but no man is so abstemious as to refuse the morning dram, which they call a skalk.'

Dr Samuel Johnson, A Journey to the Western Isles of Scotland, *1775*

Whisky takes its place

Even in Dr Johnson's time (the 1770s), many rich Scottish nobles drank claret[7] for pleasure, and many poor people made do with water, milk or beer. However, whisky – brewed by professionals in towns and by countless amateurs in the countryside – was becoming much more widely available.

Whisky even began to replace water in a number of traditional ceremonies, for example, at St Corbet's Well, near Stirling. For centuries, men and women had gathered there on May Day morning to take the waters; consuming a full glass was said to keep drinkers alive for the next 12 months. But increasingly, as the crowds grew bigger and the queues to drink grew longer, something rather stronger than water began to be taken, and people's behaviour became… well, a little bit less religious.

7. Red wine from southwest France. Since the Middle Ages, when Scotland and France had been joined together in the 'Auld Alliance' against their mutual enemy, England, Scottish traders – some permanently settled in Bordeaux – imported vast quantities of claret from France to Scotland.

66

It was said that St Corbet was not pleased. In fact, he withdrew the special powers from his well, maybe for ever! Today, the well itself seems to have disappeared. Archaeologists searching for it in 1975 could find no trace.

With so much whisky being produced – and causing disorder – it was probably inevitable that it was also going to be taxed. The first excise duty on whisky was levied by the Scottish government in 1644, to pay for Scottish troops fighting against the English.[8] For the next 200 years (almost), the history of Scottish whisky became the history of the struggle between illicit distillers and 'gaugers' (government excise officials)…

8. *Producers had to pay two shillings and eight pence (equivalent to about £10 today) per Scottish pint (around 1.5 litres.)*

Another expression of Highland single malt is about to reach the market

CHAPTER FOUR

SMUGGLERS AND EXCISEMEN

Medieval scholars[1] believed that God had kept distilled drinks away from men and women until humanity was old – and decrepit! – enough to need their restorative powers. Over the centuries, Scottish, English and, later, British governments also tried to keep whisky-making under control – though they had rather different reasons.

Most rules and regulations controlling whisky were designed to raise money. But just occasionally, governments took action simply

1. led by Catalan philosopher Ramón Llull (1232–1315).

for the public good – for example, in years of bad harvests. In the 1550s, the 1590s and again in the 1690s and 1750s, there was famine in Scotland, and even reports of cannibalism. Governments therefore banned or restricted the sale of grain for distilling, so that it could all be used to make bread.

Law and disorder

Sometimes government restrictions aimed to end lawlessness or force citizens to obey unpopular policies. A ban on whisky and wine was a central part of king James VI and I's notorious 'Highland civilisation' plan. In 1609 he invited leading Highland chieftains to sail with him on the royal ship – then refused to let them off until they had agreed to his terms. These became law, as the Statute of Icolmkill, or Iona.[2]

2. Among other things, the Statute of Iona decreed that each Highland chieftain must send his eldest son to the Lowlands to be educated, and that no chieftain's heir could inherit his father's lands if he could not speak English.

Scotland's cannibal clan?

Eighteenth-century readers of London's Newgate Calendar[3] thrilled and shivered at the story of Sawney (Alexander) Bean and his family. It didn't matter that it probably wasn't true...

Living in a huge cave on the remote coast of Galloway in southwest Scotland, Bean, his wife and their 14 children were alleged to murder unsuspecting travellers – and eat them! It was claimed that when Sawney's cave hideout was at last discovered and raided – by 400 men with bloodhounds – a goodly supply of body parts was found stored in wooden barrels. What was used to preserve them, we wonder? Possibly distilled liquor. So perhaps Sawney and his family were smugglers, as well as cannibals – or maybe wreckers?[4]

3. *A sensational work containing supposedly true stories of crime and punishment. It was named after Newgate prison in London.*
4. *Wreckers lured ships onto dangerous shores, to wreck them and steal their cargoes.*

'Barbarity, impiety and incivility...'

'One of the special causes of the great poverty of the Isles, and of the great cruelty and inhuman barbarity which has been practised by sundry of the inhabitants upon their natural friends and neighbours, has been their extraordinary drinking of strong wines and aqua vitae brought in among them, partly by merchants of the mainland and partly by traffickers among themselves.'

Statute of Iona, 1609

The Statute did not work. Not only did Islanders step up their own production of whisky to replace the banned wines, they also increased their pirate raids, attacking peaceful ships carrying alcoholic drinks and stealing their cargoes. Even chieftains were involved, though they added a veneer of respectability to their piracy by offering to buy the captured ships as 'salvage'.

Secret stills

If you were a 'barbarous' Islander, or any other small-scale producer in Scotland around 1600, how would you make whisky?

Read on, and discover whether you'd have the time, the skill and the patience...

- Choose a secluded spot for your still: up in the mountains, next to a burn (stream), and maybe close to a cattle-shieling.[5] (That will give you a good reason to be there, if anyone asks awkward questions.)

- Soak a hemp-cloth sack of barley in the burn or in a nearby bog for a couple of days.

- Spread the barley in a warm, sheltered place and leave for a week to germinate.

- Dry the sprouted barley over a smoky peat fire.

- Get the biggest container you can conveniently handle – maybe a wooden barrel.

- Put a thick layer of heather at the bottom, to act as a sieve and add a little extra flavour.

- Add the dried barley and pour on lots of boiling water. (Yes, it's hard work getting

5. shieling: a rough shelter housing women and young people who took cattle to high mountain pastures to graze in spring and summer.

73

this ready, with only a big cauldron and an open fire.) Stir very well for at least a couple of hours, and strain the mash (the sticky liquid that you've made) into another barrel.

- Add yeast, leave for 48 hours, and stand well back while the mixture heaves and bubbles.

- Now pour it into your still – a metal pot (copper is best) with a long spout or coiled 'worm'. Place the still over a brisk fire, and stand the worm in a tub of cold water (see page 39).

- While the still boils, collect the cooled alcoholic vapours as they trickle out of the worm. But don't drink them yet! To get really good whisky, you'll have to scrub out the still and distil the cooled vapours all over again.

Roderick McDonald's inn in Ross-shire may have sold whisky from rustic stills.

Money-maker

However, the most important reason for controlling the making or selling of Scotch whisky – and beer and wine and rum and brandy – was financial. At different times and in different ways, excise duties on the sale of alcoholic drinks, and/or licences to produce them, became essential sources of government income.

And yes, the wish to raise funds often conflicted with the government's other aims, such as preventing famine or maintaining law and order.

An excise timeline

The famous first reference to whisky-making in Scotland (see page 31) may also be evidence of royal licensing:

1494 Malt for making aqua vitae is supplied on the king's orders, by government officials.

Excise, duties, taxes, licences

What's the difference?

Excise: A tax levied on goods produced or sold within a country; it is specific to one particular product (e.g. whisky) or group of products (e.g. alcoholic drinks), and is usually based on a unit of measurement (e.g. gallons or barrels).

Duty: A tax levied on sales, financial transactions or property transfers, rather than on persons.

Customs duty: A tax levied on goods brought into a country.

Tax: A compulsory financial charge levied by a state; failure to pay is punishable by law. Tax is collected mostly from individuals or corporations.

Licence: Permission given by a state or other authority, often for a fixed time only; it usually has to be paid for.

Further evidence of royal policy comes just a few years later:

1505 The Surgeon-Barbers of Edinburgh are licensed by the king (James IV) as sole suppliers of aqua vitae within their city.

This royal licence is ignored, at least by some:

1550 onwards Edinburgh citizens are prosecuted for infringing the Surgeon-Barbers' monopoly.

These fines add to the Scottish government's income. But other government policies have unintended consequences that are perhaps not quite so welcome:

1550–1560 Monks are expelled from Scottish monasteries. They take their experience of distilling into the wider world. Whisky-making improves as knowledge spreads.

Next comes a terrible time. After a series of wet, cold summers, Scotland faces famine:

1579 An 'Act anent [concerning] the making of aqua vitae': the Scottish parliament bans

distilling to preserve grain for food after bad harvests. However, earls, lords, barons and gentlemen (or, rather, their servants) are still allowed to distil enough strong liquor for their own household use. Their personal stills are limited in size, as well – to a capacity of no more than 50 gallons (227 litres)!

Soon after, to reduce drunken, lawless behaviour, Scottish Islanders are banned from importing wine or aqua vitae:

1609 Statute of Iona (or Icolmkill). This law only encourages Islanders to produce more whisky for themselves – creating a whole new industry which survives until today.

It's going to take more than a law to keep an Islander from his dram. In any case, it seems as if the Statute of Iona is not working:

1616 An 'Act agens [against] the drinking of Wynes in the Yllis [Isles]'; it has to be enacted again in 1622.

In Scotland and elsewhere, the early 17th century was a time of Puritan power:

1643 The English Protestant parliament taxes imports of Scotch whisky (and much else besides) – but not for religious reasons. It's a quick way of raising money to pay for Parliament's fight against King Charles I.

Anything England can do, Scots can do better?

1644 The Scottish parliament puts the first-ever excise duty on Scottish whisky. It needs money to fight the English Royalist army.

War damages local economies:

1655 Oliver Cromwell, English Puritan leader, has taken control of Scotland. Surprisingly, he reduces duty on 'acqua vitae and strong waters' to encourage trade between Scotland and England.

New laws need new officials to enforce them, so:

1657 England appoints its first 'excise gaugers'. To begin with, they'll just check weights and measures used by distillers. Later, they'll collect excise duties – and they'll come to Scotland (see pages 82–83).

Never on a Sunday

Staunch Protestants do have their reservations about alcohol, however. In particular, they object to its being made or sold on Sundays. In 1655, farmer Robert Hage [Haig] and his wife, from a village near Stirling in Scotland, are accused of distilling on the Sabbath – a grave religious crime. In fact they have, very properly, been at church, but while their backs were turned, their 'servant lasse' has put the family still on the fire to boil, and let 'some pynts of small drink' trickle out of its long cooling arm. Mr and Mrs Haig are 'rebuked before the Session'.[6]

It's the devil's work, sure enough.

6. Session: church meeting. Distilling small quantities of whisky for household use was not illegal in Scotland at this time, although selling it was.

The war is over, but the taxes remain. Whisky duty is reduced, but:

1661 The Scottish parliament puts a new duty on malt, so as to raise money from drinkers of beer as well as whisky.

Now it's war again – first in the Highlands, near Inverness:

1689 Jacobite Highlanders burn down 'an ancient Brewary of Aquavity' at Ferintosh, belonging to Duncan Forbes of Culloden.[7] Forbes claims compensation. The Scottish parliament gives Forbes and his descendants the right to distil whisky from grain grown on his own land, free of duty.

Ferintosh, founded around 1670, is the first purpose-built Scottish distillery whose name we know.

7. *The Jacobites were the supporters of Prince James Edward Stuart, nicknamed the 'Old Pretender'. He was the son of exiled King James VII and II (forced to flee from England in 1688), and a rival claimant to William of Orange for the English and Scottish thrones. Forbes was a loyal supporter of William.*

War creates opportunities – not all of them legal, or appetising:

1690 England is fighting France. The London parliament bans the import of French wine and brandy. Scottish whisky-makers seize their opportunity, and start to smuggle whisky from Scotland to England. Tales are told of dogs with pigs' bladders full of whisky tied round their necks swimming across Border rivers.

Scotland's economy is not doing well. Its government needs more money…

1693 New duty charged on each pint of spirits sold.

1695 Malt tax is abolished, but duty on spirits increased.

God Save the Queen? Welcomed by some, hated by others, the union of Scotland with England brings many changes:

1707 The new British parliament, sitting in London, creates a new excise board for the

whole of Britain. Excise gaugers, at first mostly English, arrive in Scotland. Their task is to collect the ever-changing (and very confusing) array of duties, and to catch smugglers, arrest tax-evaders and destroy their distilleries.

But untaxed distilling and smuggling continue throughout Scotland. And dodging excisemen becomes a new national pastime.

1713 The new British excise board demands duty from the sale of malt. In Scotland the rate is 50% lower than in England. The English protest: unfair!

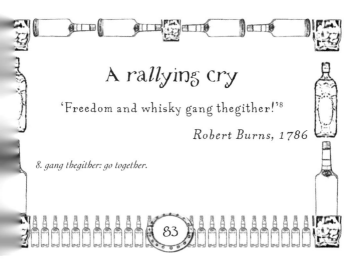

A rallying cry

'Freedom and whisky gang thegither!'[8]

Robert Burns, 1786

8. gang thegither: go together.

It's a job...

Excise gaugers were – surprise, surprise! – extremely unpopular. Why, then, did some Scotsmen agree to take on the task?

Let Scotland's favourite poet (the same one who linked whisky with freedom) explain – and apologise:

'A farm that I could live in, I could not find...
You will condemn me for the next step I have taken; I have entered the Excise.'

Letter from Robert Burns to a friend, 1788.

1725 Scottish malt duty is raised to the English rate. There are riots in Edinburgh and Glasgow. Eleven demonstrators are killed, and the MP for Glasgow has to flee for his life after his house is burned to the ground.

After the riots, even more illegal whisky stills are set up in remote areas of Scotland. And legal whisky-making increases too: by around 1730, the government receives duty on 155,000 gallons (700,000 litres) every year.

On patrol

The malt tax riots are inspired by anti-English as well as anti-excise feeling. They take place only 10 years after a Jacobite rebellion in support of Prince James Edward. The rising failed, but made the London government (and its Scottish supporters) very nervous. So government troops are stationed among Jacobites in the Highlands, to pacify – and observe – them. Are their reports true, or skewed by political prejudice? Who can say?

- 'Some…Highland gentlemen are immoderate drinkers of usky, even three or four quarts [3.5–4.5 litres] at a sitting.'

- 'In general, the people that can pay the purchase [price], drink it without moderation.'

- 'They say, for excuse, the country[9]… requires a great deal.'

- 'They pretend it does not intoxicate in the Hills as it would do in the Low country, but this…I doubt.'

Army captain Edward Burt, 1726–1727

9. the country: the harsh Highland environment.

More death and disorder, this time provoked by sympathy for smugglers:

1736 After a Scottish smuggler is hanged in Edinburgh, there are ugly riots (see opposite).

Gin, gin, gin – that's what poor people are now drinking in London. And they die from it, too – in their hundreds and thousands.

1736–1750 The British parliament taxes gin, hoping (and failing) to stop mass drunkenness. To replace it, cheap, low-quality, duty-free Scottish whisky is smuggled into England to be 'rectified'.[10]

Meanwhile, back in Scotland, there's been another rebellion. In 1745 the Jacobites rise again, this time led by 'Bonnie Prince Charlie', the Old Pretender's son. Fond of a drop of whisky himself – his all-night drinking sessions with friendly chieftains become the stuff of legend – Charlie and his troops are hopelessly out-manoeuvred. He flees to France, but his followers who remain in Scotland are savagely punished.

10. rectified: redistilled, with added flavourings.

Rough justice?

In April 1736 three well-known smugglers were sentenced to death in Edinburgh. That was the standard punishment, especially if they'd used violence to fight off excisemen. One smuggler had his sentence commuted to transportation for life, but the other two, George Robertson and Andrew Wilson, were told that they must be hanged. Helped by Wilson, Robertson managed to escape, but Wilson was executed (very horribly). The mob who saw him die were outraged, and tried to kill the hangman. Captain John Porteous (born c.1695), commander of the Edinburgh guard, stepped in to quell the riot. Rashly, he fired into the crowd, and six people died.

Porteous was arrested and tried for murder. He was found guilty, but the government in London planned to reprieve him. Furious, the Edinburgh mob attacked the Tollbooth gaol, where Porteous was imprisoned. He was dragged from his cell and lynched.

1747 Army officers at Fort Augustus (close by Loch Ness) advise troops to get their Highland prisoners drunk with whisky – the quickest way to 'penetrate their secrets'.

Bad weather strikes again:

1757 Harvests fail in Scotland. Distilling is banned for three whole years. Many duty-paying distilleries are forced out of business, but small, smugglers' distilleries thrive.

Soon, excise gaugers are given even wider powers:

1781 The government makes *all* home whisky distilling illegal, for the first time in Scotland. (Up until now, it's only been illegal to sell or export whisky without paying duties.) Is this the end of an era?

The Scots reply: 'No! Never! And to hell with the exciseman!'

The Deil's awa wi' th'Exciseman

The deil came fiddling thro' the town,
And danc'd awa' wi' th'Exciseman;
And ilka wife cries, auld Mahoun,
I wish you luck of the prize, man.

We'll mak our mau, and we'll brew our drink,
We'll laugh, sing and rejoice, man;
And mony braw thanks to the meikle black deil;
That danc'd awa' wi' th'Exciseman.

deil: devil; awa': away; wi': with; ilka: each; auld Mahoun: a nickname for the devil; mak: make; mau: malt; mony: many; braw: handsome; meikle: little.

Reluctant exciseman Robert Burns claimed that the idea for this poem came to him in 1792 as he hid in salt marshes on the shores of the Solway Firth, keeping watch for a boatload of smugglers. Possibly, the long, damp wait contributed to Burns's untimely end. He died of rheumatic heart disease just four years later, aged only 37.

By the time Burns died, over half the whisky made in Scotland was distilled illegally. Most of it came from the Highlands. But that was rapidly changing…

Whisky became big business in the 18th century

CHAPTER FIVE

'A MOST RASCALLY LIQUOR'[1]

By around 1770, just one distillery – Ferintosh, on the Black Isle near Inverness – was producing almost two-thirds of the 'legal' whisky in Scotland.[2] The Ferintosh ouput was a very impressive 90,000 gallons (409,000 litres) every year, and it was reckoned to be good quality. But it was nothing like enough to meet the demand from whisky drinkers in Scotland, or elsewhere. So illegal stills, large and small, flourished wherever they could be hidden. And Scottish

1. *Robert Burns, referring to new* Lowland *whisky.*
2. *As we saw on page 81, its owners, the Forbes family, had been exempted from paying duty in 1689. They were by now very rich indeed, and had built three more distilleries.*

entrepreneurs began to build big new, legal distilleries in the Lowlands, to supply a new mass market in Scotland's fast-growing industrial towns and cities.

Ferintosh was the first purpose-built distillery to be named in Scottish documents, in 1689. By 1824, many others had been recorded:

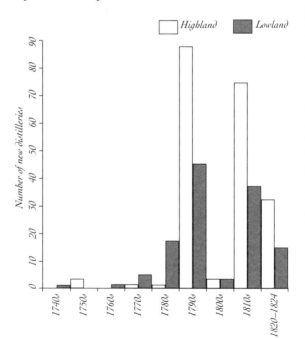

Big business

Appropriately enough, these new distilleries were often rather like factories. The largest was Kilbagie, near Alloa in the Scottish Central Lowlands, opened around 1770. It employed 500 men, and had its own mills to thresh and grind grain for malting. It used 60,000 bolls (about 3,810 tonnes) of grain per year; and the draff (leftovers from brewing the mash) was enough to feed 7,000 bullocks and 2,000 pigs. Its buildings – some an impressive four storeys tall – covered 2 hectares; it had its own freshwater stream, and its own canal. Barges full of grain docked there, then left laden with full barrels. At its peak in the late 1780s, Kilbagie claimed to be producing 5,000 tons (5.1 million litres) of Lowland whisky every year.

Distilleries like Kilbagie were owned and run by a new breed of Scottish businessmen, nicknamed 'whisky barons'. Two of the greatest, James Stein and John Haig, belonged to the same extended family. Together they controlled almost half the legal whisky production in Scotland.

GIGO
(Garbage in, garbage out)

The Steins and the Haigs were very proud of their whisky. But, to cut costs and increase production, other new Lowland distilleries brewed their mash from mediocre mixed grains. 'Reject' wheat and unmalted barley were the most usual, although all kinds of other substances were also used on occasion.

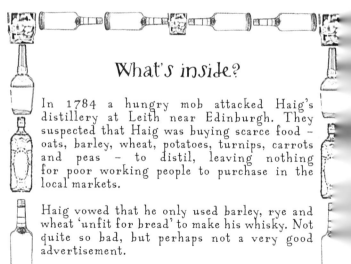

What's inside?

In 1784 a hungry mob attacked Haig's distillery at Leith near Edinburgh. They suspected that Haig was buying scarce food – oats, barley, wheat, potatoes, turnips, carrots and peas – to distil, leaving nothing for poor working people to purchase in the local markets.

Haig vowed that he only used barley, rye and wheat 'unfit for bread' to make his whisky. Not quite so bad, but perhaps not a very good advertisement.

To reduce their costs still further, many new Lowland distilleries churned out every last drop of spirit that they could, fast and furiously. One stillman boasted of being able to 'work off' (empty) a still in just 15 minutes.[3] Compared with legal Ferintosh, or the output of the best illegal distillers, the whisky produced in this hasty, brutal way was thin, sharp, harsh, bitter, and burning, 'only fitted for the most vulgar… palates'. Understandably, it became the fashion to drink it with water, sugar and lemons, to hide the taste. And unlike today, where top-quality whiskies may be matured for 12 years or much more, this Lowland whisky – and some Highland whisky, too – was drunk fresh from the still. Glasgow whisky-sellers proudly advertised their receipt of 'new' deliveries, fresh from the distillers, aged about 6 weeks!

In spite of the rude things said about the new Lowland whisky, it was consumed in vast quantities. In Govan (now part of Glasgow), 279 factory workers' families were said to have drunk 6,000 gallons (27,300 litres) between them in one year.

3. Today, an average still takes about 6 hours to run.

Profits – and taxes

Why did the Lowland distillers sacrifice quality to quantity?

• Partly because large amounts of cheap whisky – about 184,000 gallons (835,000 litres) in 1782 – were shipped south to England, where it was either redistilled into gin, or sold to poor working men who could not afford anything better. English distillers complained, with good reason, that the Lowland Scots were deliberately trying to put them out of business.

• And partly because making quick, mass-produced whisky was a way of outwitting the exciseman. In the early 1780s, duty was levied on the notional output of each still, not on its actual production. So the more whisky that was made, the smaller the proportion of a company's total profits had to be handed over as duty. To try to collect what they believed they were 'really' owed by distillers, governments increased the duty on whisky-making and tried new ways of assessing it.

The most momentous change came in 1784, when the British parliament passed the 'Wash Act'. This divided Scotland into a Highland zone and a Lowland zone, each with entirely different rules for whisky-making.

farewell ferintosh?

At the same time (1784), the Forbes family at Ferintosh lost its former privileges, and had to pay for a licence like all other Highland whisky producers.

> Thee Ferintosh! O sadly lost!
> Scotland laments from coast to coast!
> Now colic-grips an' barkin' hoast
>   May kill us a',
> For loyal Forbes's chartered boast
>   Is ta'en awa.

colic-grips: stomach pains; hoast: cough; a': all; ta'en awa': taken away.

Poetically speaking, not one of Robert Burns's best efforts, perhaps, but written from the heart, in 1786.

You take the high road...

In the Highland zone, whisky distillers could pay for an annual licence, based on the supposed capacity of their still(s). They were then free of excise duty on their whisky, so long as they had used only local-grown barley. There was, of course, only a limited amount of Highland barley available; the government thought that this would put a natural limit on Highland whisky production. Furthermore, after 1814, Highland distillers were no longer allowed to sell whisky outside the Highland zone. The government hoped that restricting the market in this way would also help dry up Highland whisky production.

...and I'll take the low road

In the Lowland zone, by contrast, distillers were taxed on each gallon of wash (see page 118) that they actually produced. Duty on Lowland whisky was fixed at the same rate as that paid by English gin distillers. This was unfair, since it took much more wash to make a bottle of whisky than a bottle of gin.

Another new law, in 1786, aimed to remove this injustice but still make money for the Excise. Now legal Lowland distillers had to pay a licence fee like the Highlanders, plus an extra duty on whisky exports. Once again, they tried to recover the extra costs of these taxes by producing more liquor, extra-cheaply. They built new wide, flat-bottomed stills that took just minutes to work off – and Lowland whisky output rose yet again. But these stills soon burned out and had to be replaced; they also needed a lot of fuel to run them. By 1788, profit margins for distillers were perilously narrow.

Duty up, output up

In 1788 the duty on whisky exports was raised once more, and the licence fee also. Lowland distillers were told to give 12 months' notice of their intention to export whisky (to give excisemen the chance to check up on them) – but this halted their trade for a whole year. Many big Lowland businesses went bankrupt, including the Haigs and the Steins (though they were able to start up again soon after). And the Excise lost a lot of money, too: in

1788 Haig and Stein owed them £700,000 (equivalent to about £40 million today).

When Britain went to war with Napoleon's France in 1793, the government had a further reason – or excuse – for increasing duties (and they did so again in 1795, 1800, 1803 and 1811!). Also in wartime, no French wine or brandy could be imported – which meant increased demand for whisky. Finally, in 1814, the government banned all stills under 500 gallons (2,273 litres) in the Highlands. If obeyed, this new law would have meant an end to Highland whisky production.

A golden age – for smugglers

What could distillers do? For many, there was only one answer: go illegal! Unintentionally, between 1707 and 1814 the British government had created ideal conditions to encourage whisky smuggling. Buying duty-free whisky from unlicensed stills became so common that it was considered completely respectable. As the son of one Highland laird remembered, looking back to the 1820s, 'My father never tasted any but smuggled whisky.'

Get the best

Illegal Highland whisky was also much better than most legal Lowland products. It had an excellent reputation:

'In several of the most solitary glens, we saw the caves where the smugglers manufacture the famous Highland whisky, which is so far superior to the ordinary, by being distilled from the pure malt and smoked with the peat.'

Wealthy English tourist, 1812

Thanks to bold, bad smugglers, illegal whisky was available everywhere:

'They travel in bands of 50 or 80 or 150 horses remarkably stout and fleet and having the audacity to go in the open day upon the public high roads and through the streets of...towns and villages.'

Government report, 1790

And almost everyone welcomed it:

'The skill displayed cheating the Revenue is regarded rather as proof of praiseworthy dexterity than as a crime.'

James Loch, Factor to the Duke of Sutherland (1780–1855)

Top tips for smugglers

- Carry a wooden cudgel – a big one. Or, if you can afford it, buy a gun. But beware: if you kill an exciseman, you'll be hanged for murder. Self defence – some excisemen fight back tough and dirty – is no excuse!

- Travel by night, unless you're one of a large gang – in which case no-one will dare challenge you even in daytime.

- Use trusty, sure-footed Highland ponies. They can swim across rivers and splash through bogs, and withstand bitter winds and weather. Two barrels, one each side, to balance them, is their usual load.

- Post lookouts and sentries – or else make use of nature. If you build your still near a rookery, the birds will swoop and caw if anyone approaches.

- Try a decoy expedition. Send out a couple of old men with a feeble horse laden with empty barrels. The excisemen will chase after them – and you can safely carry your smuggled load in the opposite direction.

- Hide your still in a cave, or underwater. And the spray from a waterfall will usefully disguise the smoke from your still. In cities, stills can be hidden in cellars, under bridges, in graveyards or even in clock towers.

- Your local minister may help you. Smuggled whisky has been hidden under pulpits or in coffins before now.

- Got a 'hot' wee barrel at home? You could bury it in the garden, or hide it in a big tub of flour.

- Last but not least, get a wife! Best would be a tall, strong woman who can carry a made-to-measure metal 'jacket' under her stays or a curved canister beneath her skirts – that's often done. Or else be like one man we've heard of, who dresses up a barrel of smuggled whisky in women's clothes, with a veil, and gets his servant to tie it behind him once he's seated on his horse.

Are ye all right back there, hen?

No choice!

Yes, Highlanders were breaking the law, but, as almost everyone pointed out, they simply had to do it. Illegal distilling was the only way in which poor families could earn enough cash to pay their rent and buy oatmeal to make their bannocks (oatcakes). There were no shops or factories in most villages, and small-scale sheep and cattle farming had never been very profitable:

'Tomintoul [a remote village]... is inhabited by 37 families, without a single manufacture... all of them sell whisky and all of them drink it.'

Church of Scotland Minister, 1790

Almost everyone bought Highland whisky, too, from rich lairds to poor crofters, from righteous ministers to corrupt local magistrates. As one Campbeltown woman distiller indignantly complained in court to the justice who admonished her:

'But I haven't made a drop since that wee keg I sent you last week!'

By around 1800, there were close on 14,000 illicit stills in the Highlands – and a great many smugglers. There were even coppersmiths in Highland towns like Inverness who advertised their skills at making and mending home distillery equipment by boldly hanging signs outside their workshops.

Auld Reekie[4]

Hundreds of illegal distillers were working away in Scotland's grimy, crowded cities and towns. It was easy to hide the smoke from a still among the reeking house and factory chimneys. It was said that in the late 1700s Edinburgh had 400 stills, but only 8 of them were legal.

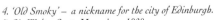

Mine own
romantic town[5]...
alcoholic

4. 'Old Smoky' – a nickname for the city of Edinburgh.
5. Sir Walter Scott, Marmion, 1808.

Why be an exciseman?

Faced with such universal opposition to government licences and taxes, an exciseman's task looked impossible. And his hours were long, his work was hard, his pay was poor, and the risks were considerable. He could not always rely on magistrates to help him, and, almost everywhere, he was deeply unpopular.

Some excisemen, like Burns, could not find another job and badly needed the money. Some may have been inspired by a sense of public duty. Some, like famous excise officer Malcolm Gillespie, who lived and worked near Aberdeen, seem to have enjoyed the thrill of the chase, and pitting their wits against smugglers.

In a career lasting 28 years, Gillespie boasted of seizing 6,535 gallons (29,710 litres) of whisky, plus 62,400 gallons (283,700 litres) of undistilled wash (presumably by catching distillers red-handed). He impounded 85 carts, 165 horses and 407 illegal stills. For a while he was helped by his fearsome bull-terrier, which he trained to bite smugglers' horses. But a smuggler shot it dead – and Gillespie himself suffered at least 40 serious injuries. Strangely, his death came, not in a smugglers' fight, but after he himself was caught law-breaking. He was hanged in 1827, for forgery.

Royal – and ridiculous

In 1822 King George IV of Great Britain was persuaded to pay a state visit to Scotland. He was most impressed. He wore a kilt (with pink woollen tights underneath), and, naturally, he requested a dram of good Scottish whisky. An anxious message was rushed to the king's advisers. 'What kind of whisky would the king like to drink?' 'Why, Glenlivet!' It was his favourite.

Glenlivet was indeed good whisky – the top choice of many Scottish nobles. But it was made in the Highlands! It was strictly illegal! It could only be got from smugglers!

Did King George break the law and get his drink? Yes – and he enjoyed it. And he rewarded the nobleman who supplied the Glenlivet with a top royal appointment.

Clearly this ridiculous state of affairs could not continue. Illegal distilling must be controlled, and royalty could not be seen to break its own laws quite so publicly. Parliament decided to act (yet again!)…

A touch of the Orient? The 'pagoda' roof of the malt kiln provides ventilation to help dry the malt

CHAPTER SIX

NEW LAWS, NEW TECHNOLOGY

he modern Scotch whisky industry dates from 1823. That is when the duke of Gordon (whose estates included a large number of illegal Highland distilleries) pressed for a new law: the Excise Act. It allowed the legal distilling of whisky in return for an annual licence fee of £10 (equivalent to around £420 today), plus a fixed fee per gallon of proof spirit produced.

After 1823, smuggling was no longer worth the risk, especially as the new act imposed savage penalties for illegal distilling. New, legal distilleries were set up in the Highlands

and the Lowlands – often at remote sites used by illicit stills in the past, which is why some of today's malt-whisky distilleries are in such beautiful surroundings. Output soared from around 13 million litres to 45 million litres between 1823 and 1828. And in just two years, from 1823 to 1825, over 200 new distilleries were licensed in Scotland.

By now, whisky-making had developed its own special technology – based on traditional stills, but designed to produce much larger volumes than the old secret Highland stills – and its own baffling vocabulary…

Smugglers' revenge

One of the first of the new legal distilleries was in the famous valley of Glenlivet (see page 107), where around 200 small, illegal distilleries had been sited. Its owner was George Smith, who came from a famous (illegal) distilling family. His former smuggler comrades objected strongly – and threatened to burn the new distillery down.

Weird whisky words

What's got body, and a nose, and length and strength and character, but needs maturing and finishing?

Yes, you've guessed, it's whisky! Check this list and see how many other weird and wonderful whisky words you know.

Barrel A small wooden cask, typically containing about 200 litres (but definitions vary).

Bere A prehistoric variety of barley that grows in Scotland, traditionally said to be the best for making whisky.

Bond or **bonded warehouse** A building where whisky on which excise duty has not yet been paid is stored under lock and key.

Caramel Burnt sugar solution, sometimes used to colour whisky.

Cask A wooden container in which newly distilled whisky is stored to mature.

Condenser A large container in which alcoholic vapours rising from a still are trapped, chilled and returned to a liquid state. The traditional **worm** is one type of condenser. In the 20th century many distilleries installed larger, faster shell-and-tube condensers. These consist of many lengths of copper tubing packed into a metal case (the 'shell'), through which cold water is kept running.

STEEPING   MALTING   GRINDING

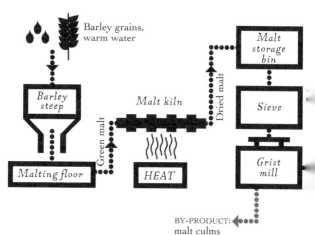

Barley grains, warm water

Barley steep

Malting floor

Green malt

Malt kiln

HEAT

Dried malt

Malt storage bin

Sieve

Grist mill

BY-PRODUCT: malt culms

Congeners Tiny traces of naturally occurring chemicals (the by-products of fermentation) remaining in whisky after distillation. They help give it a characteristic colour, scent and flavour – and are also said to cause hangovers.

Copper The metal used to make whisky stills. It improves the wash and the low wines by interacting with and removing sulphur-containing compounds.

Draff What is left of the grist after mashing has finished. It is used to feed cattle.

Dressing Shaking or sieving the kiln-dried malt

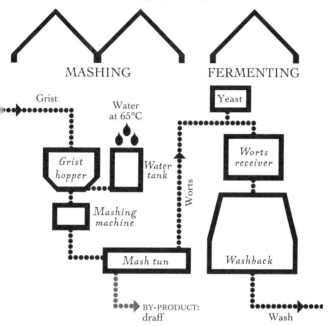

MASHING

FERMENTING

Grist

Water at 65°C

Yeast

Grist hopper

Water tank

Worts receiver

Mashing machine

Worts

Mash tun

Washback

BY-PRODUCT: draff

Wash

to remove the dead rootlets before it is ground into grist.

Feints Unpleasant, heavy alcohols, left after the middle cut has been taken from the spirit still. They are later redistilled with the low wines.

Feints receiver A large tank for collecting and storing feints from a spirit still, ready for redistilling.

Fermentation A biological reaction between yeast and a sugar, for example, the malt sugars found in wash. The yeast feeds on the sugar, giving off alcohol and carbon dioxide.

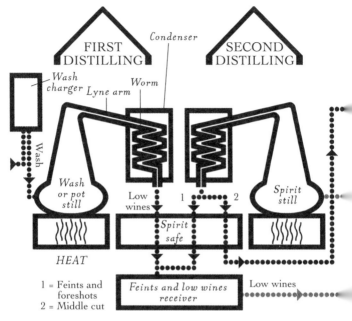

FIRST DISTILLING

Condenser

SECOND DISTILLING

Wash charger

Lyne arm

Worm

Wash

Wash or pot still

Low wines

Spirit still

1   2

HEAT

Spirit safe

1 = Feints and foreshots
2 = Middle cut

Feints and low wines receiver

Low wines

Fermentation vessel   Another name for a washback.

Foreshots   The light, pungent, first alcohols to vaporise during distillation in a spirit still. They are not suitable for human consumption, and are collected in the feints receiver to be redistilled, along with the feints and the low wines.

Green malt   Steeped barley grains that have grown rootlets.

Grist   Ground, dried malt ready for mashing. Until the 1880s, malt was ground between millstones. Since then, it has been ground by steel rollers.

MATURING

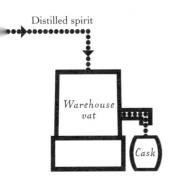

Distilled spirit

Warehouse vat

Cask

Casks in warehouse

Grist hopper A large raised container in which grist is stored, ready to be poured into the mash tun.

Low wines The larger part of the alcoholic liquid produced after distilling the wash in a wash still. It is stored in a large vat called the **low wines charger** (or **receiver**) until it can be pumped to the spirit still for second distillation.

Lyne arm or **lye pipe** A sloping tube that leads from the top of a wash still or spirit still to a worm or condenser.

Malt Grains of barley that have been germinated

(made to sprout) then dried to produce a sweet, sugary substance.

Malt culms or **combings** The dead rootlets removed from green malt after it has been dried; sold as cattle feed.

Malting floor A slatted or perforated floor where steeped grains of barley are spread out and raked over. After 5–10 days they grow rootlets, and the starch they contain is converted into sugar. They are now called **green malt**.

Maltings The building where steeped grains are turned into green malt.

Malt kiln The furnace where green malt grains are dried at 60°C for two days, sometimes over smoke. This is called 'kilning the malt'.

Mash house The building where mashing takes place.

Mashing Mixing grist and boiling water, then stirring the mixture to produce a sugary liquid known as **wort** or **worts**. Mashing is repeated up to four times with each batch of grist.

Mashing machine A vessel in which grist is mixed with boiling water before entering the mash tun.

Mash tun A huge tub (up to 36,000 litres) in which grist and water at 65°C are stirred together. It is usually made of stainless steel.

Middle cut The central fraction of alcoholic liquid made by distilling low wines in a spirit still. It is the part of the distilled liquid that eventually becomes whisky.

Peat reek A smoky flavour produced by drying malt over peat.

Phenols Chemicals in peat smoke (and elsewhere) that smell smoky, tarry or antiseptic. They give some whiskies their flavour. Lightly peated

whisky has about 2 ppm (parts per million) of phenols; medium-peated whisky has about 25 ppm, and heavily peated whisky around 35–50 ppm.

Pot ale   Dregs left after the wash has been distilled; mixed with draff to make cattle feed.

Reflux   Alcoholic vapour that condenses before it reaches the lyne arm and runs back into the still. Some say that reflux contributes to a whisky's final character.

Silent season   High summer, when, traditionally, whisky was not made.

Spargeing   The final stage of mashing: mixing the last tunful of water with a batch of grist and heating it.

Spent lees   Any residue left in the spirit safe after distillation is over.

Spirit receiver   The container in which the middle cut is stored as it leaves the spirit safe.

Spirit safe   A locked glass box through which newly distilled alcoholic liquor is piped as it leaves the spirit still. The stillman can observe its condition, judge when to stop and start collecting the middle cut, and use valves to direct the foreshots, middle cut and feints to their separate receivers.

Steep   To soak grains of barley until they soften, swell and germinate (begin to shoot).

Still   A large copper vessel in which wash is distilled to produce whisky. There are two kinds: **wash stills** distil wash in the first distillation, and **spirit stills** distil low wines in the second distillation.

Swan's neck   The part of the lyne arm that bends and begins to slope downwards.

Underback Another name for **worts receiver**.

Wash Wort to which yeast has been added to make a beer-like substance.

Washback A huge vessel, made of pinewood or stainless steel, in which wort is mixed with yeast and left for around 36 hours to ferment. The fermentation can be very violent, so washbacks have to be bolted securely to the floor. To prevent overflowing, manual or mechanical **switchers** (beaters) are used to break down the froth (or **barm**) that develops on top of the wash.

Wash receiver The container that holds fermented wash once it has been pumped out of the washback, ready for first distilling.

Water Chemically speaking, whisky is made with ordinary water (H_2O), but where it flows – through peat, over granite – has been terribly important to whisky-makers. So has its degree of hardness (alkalinity) or softness (acidity). Modern chemists say that water quality should make no difference to the finished drink, but some whisky experts disagree.

Worm A coiled copper tube, traditionally used to condense alcoholic vapours after first and second distillations. Mostly now replaced by shell-and-tube condensers.

Worm tub A wood or metal tub full of cold, flowing water, traditionally used to cool alcoholic vapours as they passed through worms.

Wort or **worts** A syrupy liquid made by mashing grist and water together.

Worts receiver The large container into which the strained worts runs after mashing has finished.

Choose your grains!

So far in this book, we have been mostly talking about malt whisky. (Apart from dubious concoctions made by some early Lowland distillers (see pages 94–95), there really wasn't any other kind.) But today, as we know, there are many different types of whisky, made from all kinds of different grains. How did they come to be made?

Largely thanks to an Irishman, one Aeneas Coffey. He was Dublin's Chief Excise Officer, but was also keenly interested in all technical aspects of making whisky. In 1831 he perfected a new 'Patent (or Coffey) Still' (also called a 'column still'). It was based on an earlier (1826) invention by Scotsman Robert Stein, a member of the famous Haig and Stein Lowland distilling dynasty.

The Coffey process

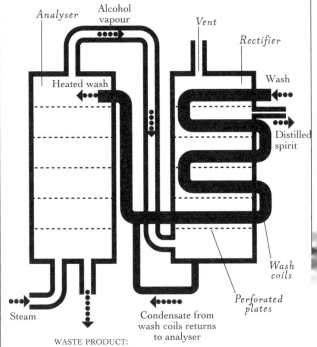

The Coffey still consists of two columns, the analyser and the rectifier, connected by pipes. Each column contains a stack of perforated metal plates or trays.

In the analyser, hot wash is pumped in at the top and steam at the bottom. The steam makes the wash boil on the surface of the plates, and alcohol vapours collect at the top of the analyser.

The alcohol vapours from the analyser are pumped into the bottom of the rectifier. Some of the vapour condenses on the wash coils and is recycled back into the analyser. The rest of the vapour collects at the top of the rectifier. This vapour then goes through a condenser, where it cools and becomes liquid spirit. The distilled spirit then flows through a spirit safe, where it is checked for strength and purity, as in the malt-whisky method described earlier.

Transformed by technology

Haig's and Coffey's new stills revolutionised the distilling process, for whisky and for other alcoholic beverages. Firstly, and quite unlike traditional malt-whisky stills, they allowed good-quality alcohol to be distilled from a wide variety of grains. These could be distilled alone or, if the makers chose, combined with a proportion of traditional malted barley.

How did the new stills do this? By cooking the grains, usually with steam, at the very start of the process. Like malting, this enabled natural sugars to develop. The grains could then be mixed with water to make worts, and yeast could be added to make wash. After that, the distillation was similar to that of malt whisky. But there was a very important difference: the spirit made by these new patent stills needed to be distilled only once, not twice.

Single distillation meant that patent stills could be kept running continually, to produce a constant flow at regular alcoholic strength and steady, predictable quality. This was not only quicker than the traditional way of distilling malt whisky; it was also considerably cheaper.

Traditionalists were doubtful: was this new product really whisky? But many distillers were delighted. Now whisky could be made on a larger scale than ever before – and, hopefully, so could profits!

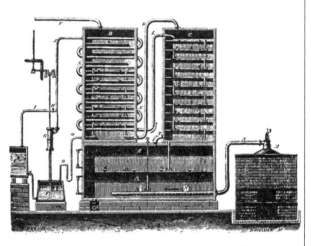

Engraving of a Coffey still
c. 1870

CHAPTER SEVEN

BARRELS, BOTTLES, BLENDS, BRANDS – AND BUGS

Sadly, almost half the new distilleries set up after the 1823 Excise Act did not survive for long. Around 100 were already closed by 1840. Some had been too small; some had been badly run; some had been sabotaged by former smugglers. Together, they had also, we might say, flooded the market. Malt whisky was not yet widely drunk outside Scotland. And, keen though Scots men – and women – were to consume their national drink, even they had their limits. There was just too much malt whisky to go round.

A decent dram

'At every house it was offered…from early
morning till late at night it [whisky-drinking]
went on. Decent gentlewomen began the day
with a dram.'

Elizabeth Grant, Memoirs of a Highland Lady
*(published 1898 but looking back to
earlier in the century)*

At the same time, the British government was
steadily increasing the excise duty levied on
whisky – by almost 50% between 1824 and
1830. This led to old, illegal stills being started
up again, falling sales for legal distilleries –
and less money collected in duty for
the government. Legal distillers and MPs
were united: 'Something must be done!'
A parliamentary commission investigated
from 1831 to 1836, but came to no very helpful
conclusions.

In the Lowlands, meanwhile, the grain-whisky business was booming – especially after cheap, duty-free maize, imported from America, became available in the 1850s. Like earlier Lowland whisky, most of the new grain spirit produced by the Coffey stills (see pages 119–123) was sent to England to be redistilled as gin, or sold in Scotland and England to poor working people.

Very tasty!

Pub landlord or spirit-seller in a poor part of town? Got a job lot of cheap and disgusting grain whisky to get rid of? Do you want to 'add value' to it, as they say? Try these tasty additives:

- glycerine
- varnish
- turpentine
- prunes
- acetic acid
- burnt sugar
- whole pineapple
- naphtha
- green tea
- sulphuric acid

They probably won't kill your customers. But if they do, you can always blame the alcohol in the whisky!

All these adulterations, and more, were exposed by campaigning journalists in 1872.

friends and enemies

Grain distillers were also mixing some of their cheap, rather tasteless whisky with strong-flavoured malt whisky, and selling it at much lower prices than traditional malt distilleries could charge. This led to bitter quarrels, nicknamed 'whisky wars', between grain and malt distillers. They lasted throughout the 19th century.

There was also intense rivalry between grain distillery firms. To prevent fierce price-cutting putting them all out of business, from 1856 grain distillers joined together in trade associations, agreeing to share the market with each other. Later, in 1877, many of the largest grain distillers formed the Distillers Company Limited. It was led – according to the new company secretary – by a team of powerful whisky barons: 'the determined Haig, the politic Bald, the impetuous Mcfarlane, the subtle Mowbray, the anxious Stewart, the cautious MacNab and the bold Menzies'.

Way out west

For hard-pressed malt distillers there was, however, a glimmer of hope on the horizon. Sales to new markets overseas were increasing, especially to the USA. After 1846 they were boosted by the ending of high export duties, as government policies encouraged Free Trade.[1] Malt whisky began to be sold all round the world. It was very soon joined by bottled, branded blends.

1. Even so, there were still some difficulties. The long sea voyage to tropical climates did nothing to improve whisky's flavour. At least one shipload of whisky proved undrinkable when it reached India, and had to be thrown overboard.

Scotland's five whisky-producing regions
(legally recognised since 2009)

Orkney

HIGHLAND

SPEYSIDE

Inverness

Aberdeen

Dundee

Glasgow

Edinburgh

ISLAY

LOWLAND

CAMPBELTOWN

ENGLAND

It's progress!

Sales of whisky outside Scotland were also helped by Victorian advances in faster, cheaper transport (railways and steamships), cheap, colourful printing (newspaper advertisements and posters), and cheaper, clever and more convenient packaging technology.

From 1860 it was legal to sell whisky – good, bad or indifferent – in single bottles, rather than only in bulk as before. Bottles could be filled on factory mass-production lines, plastered with eye-catching labels and fitted with reusable cork stoppers. Now, for the first time, 'respectable' ordinary people could afford to keep a bottle of whisky in the sideboard. They could pour 'a stiff peg' in emergencies or sip 'just a little' to celebrate special occasions.

Whisky in the jar

If you wanted to buy whisky at any time before 1860, you had few options:

- If you were rich, you bought a barrel or a hogshead or a puncheon or even a butt – all names for different sizes of the wooden casks in which whisky was sold, duty-paid, by distillery companies. Or you purchased a pottery jar, containing between 8 and 10 gallons (36–45 litres), from a specialist wine and spirit merchant.

- If you were poor, you took a jug or any other suitable receptacle to be filled at your nearest licensed grocery or public house.[2] Then you carried your purchase home very gently, trying not to spill a precious drop.

- Whisky was also sold by the glass, at licensed pubs, bars and hotels.

2. Or, in Scotland or Ireland, you went to the nearest illegal still, though there were fewer and fewer of these. Only 19 were discovered by Scottish excisemen in 1854.

That's my whisky!

What sort of whisky did these new mass-market consumers choose to drink at home, or order in a bar? Almost always a branded blend that they could recognise by its bottle shape or label, and ask for by name. The first known blend, Usher's Old Vatted Glenlivet, was created by Edinburgh merchant Andrew Usher in 1853. He combined smoky, heathery Highland malts with softer, gentler malts distilled in the Lowlands.

After 1860, the law allowed malt and grain whiskies to be blended together and sold as 'whisky'. Many of the world's best-known brands were created in this way. They include:

- White Horse
- Johnnie Walker
- Dewar's
- Black & White
- Haig
- Vat 69
- Bell's

Most blends contained a large proportion of light, neutral grain whisky, with smaller amounts of several different, strongly flavoured malts. When skilfully composed, blended whisky could be very good. It could (or should) also be trusted to be free from additives – and each batch of a blend always tasted the same. Once purchasers found a blend they liked, they could go on buying it, hopefully, for a lifetime. As an added bonus for distillers and customers, blends were cheaper to produce and purchase than pure malt whisky.[3]

All this was very good news for distillers' sales and profits. So, from the 1860s to the 1890s, a new generation of whisky barons, most famously the flamboyant Tommy Dewar (1864–1930), worked hard to find new markets and create appealing identities for their own branded blends.

Even malt-whisky distillers recognised the importance of branding – and brand integrity. In a famous law case in 1880, distiller John Gordon Smith fought for the right to call his product '*The* Glenlivet' – and won.

---

3. They made use of whiskies that might have been undrinkable on their own. There were also economies of scale: wholesale blenders could produce whisky to be sold as several different brands.

Bright ideas

If you were a go-ahead whisky salesman, which of these ideas would you choose to spearhead your marketing campaign?

- Cause a public nuisance by playing the bagpipes, then make maximum use of the publicity that follows.

- Train 500 parrots to say 'Pattison's is best'.[4]

- Dress all the time like a music-hall star – in top hat and tails – then persuade music halls to sell only your brand.

- Do deals with captains of cargo ships to sell your whisky overseas.

- Become whisky supplier to the House of Commons.

- Drive everywhere in a super-smart carriage pulled by a beautifully matched pair of horses.

- Appeal to sportsmen! Show horses and riders in your publicity.

- Strike a patriotic note! Include soldiers and guns and heroes in your advertisements.

Scots whisky barons tried all these tactics – and, surprisingly, they worked.

4. Or something like that – reports vary.

Old, older, oldest

Today, by law, Scotch whisky has to be at least three years old.[5] But until the mid-19th century, almost all whisky was sold fresh from the still, and purchasers kept unopened casks at home for as long as they chose. But by the late 19th century, blended whisky – and soon many other whiskies, as well – were bottled and sold only after being 'matured'.

Age – and the smoothness it was said to bring[6] – became powerful selling points. Maturing changed clear, colourless new whisky to the widely advertised 'amber nectar'. It mellowed the sharp, fiery bite of alcohol, and let new flavours develop as all the different elements in each cask reacted with each other, and with the air.

5. That is, it has to be stored in the cask for three years after distilling. The law was introduced during World War I in an attempt to cut down drunkenness among the troops. Older whisky was more expensive, so – law-makers hoped – soldiers would drink less of it.
6. Nineteenth-century Irish whiskey was famous for being more smooth and delicate than 'rough Scots'. This led to one Edinburgh distillery – the Caledonian – claiming that it produced 'Irish' whisky 'precisely similar to that made in Dublin'. Scottish and Irish whiskies were also sold blended together.

Thirsty work, being holy...

Wooden casks weren't (and still aren't) completely airtight, so a certain amount[7] of whisky evaporated as it was left in them to mature. Because alcohol vapour is lighter than air, it rose upwards, towards the heavens – so it was nicknamed 'the angels' share'.

It's not that I begrudge them their share, Carruthers – I just wonder why they need it.

7. British Customs and Excise assumed 2% every year.

Sensory

Today, food scientists and whisky experts have developed a systematic method of describing all the different scents and tastes in matured whisky.

They call it 'sensory analysis' and display it on a 'flavour wheel'.

Oil

Rotten eggs

Rubber

Metal

Old books

Sherry

Vinegar

Spice

SULPHUR

WINE

Vanilla

Caramel

Nuts

Pine disinfectant

Sawdust

WOOD

FEINTS

Plastic

Cheese

Sweat

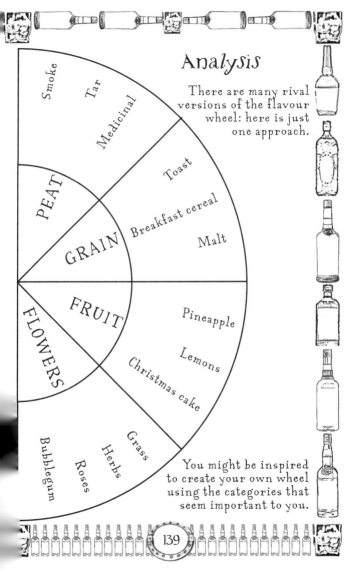

Analysis

There are many rival versions of the flavour wheel: here is just one approach.

PEAT
- Smoke
- Tar
- Medicinal

GRAIN
- Toast
- Breakfast cereal
- Malt

FRUIT
- Pineapple
- Lemons
- Christmas cake

FLOWERS
- Grass
- Herbs
- Roses
- Bubblegum

You might be inspired to create your own wheel using the categories that seem important to you.

Scotland the brand!
Design your own whisky poster

Here's how to create an authentic poster or label for your own brand of Scotch whisky:

1. Copy or cut out these pictures and assemble them on a sheet of paper in any way you like.

2. Scatter a few Scottish words around.

3. Stand back and toast your creation in – what else? – Scotch whisky!

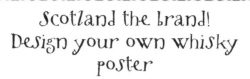

GLEN

dram

BRAE

frae the Hielands

Och Aye!

LOCH

SPECIAL BLEND

By Royal Appointment

In the second half of the century, whisky marketeers also received help from two rather unlikely sources: ultra-respectable Queen Victoria – and a louse from America!

'Every year my heart becomes more fixed on this dear paradise.' So wrote Queen Victoria about her royal holiday home at Balmoral in Aberdeenshire. Her Majesty's love affair with all things Highland began in 1848, when she paid her first visit to Balmoral. That started a fashion for Scottish holidays among the British Empire's upper classes – and also helped to popularise Highland malt whisky.

In 1848, shortly after arriving on her first trip to Balmoral, Queen Victoria paid a visit, with Prince Albert and the royal children, to the Lochnagar distillery nearby. The royal party inspected its impressive machinery, and then sampled the whisky. They seem to have liked it, and ordered supplies, because the owner was appointed Distiller to the Queen, and allowed to call his – now very fashionable – whisky 'Royal Lochnagar'.

Six-legged – and nasty!

In 1870, wine-makers in France noticed something strange and extremely alarming. Their precious vines were turning brown, and withering, and shrivelling. There were no new shoots, no green leaves, no grapes to make wine. It was a disaster!

It was indeed. A tiny aphid-like insect, *Phylloxera vastatrix*, had migrated from America. It attacked and killed grapevines, halting wine production throughout Europe for years. Without wine, there was no brandy; and so, for whisky distillers, the *Phylloxera* attack became a blessing in disguise. Their marketing teams persuaded the upper classes in England and elsewhere that blended whisky would be just the thing to replace their favourite – but unobtainable – brandy and soda. Sales soared, and the 1880s and 1890s saw a 'Whisky Boom'.

The demon Drink

Not everyone was pleased by whisky's growing popularity. The Temperance Movement (founded 1829) urged its members to 'totally abstain' from all alcohol. It won supporters throughout the United Kingdom, even in Scotland. And it inspired a positive torrent of newspaper articles, pamphlets – and, erm, poetry:

'O thou demon Drink, thou fell destroyer;
Thou curse of society, and its great annoyer;
What hast thou done to society, let me think?
I answer thou hast caused the most of ills,
        thou demon Drink.'

Dundee's own, very own, William Topaz McGonagall (1825–1902)

On the other hand...

Whisky distillers had a ready reply to Temperance tracts: 'Drink up! It's your patriotic duty!' In many ways, at least for rural Scotland, this was true. Whisky was now a leading force in the Scottish economy. Arable farmers depended on growing barley for brewers and distillers; Lowland cattle farms also relied on 'draff' (spent grain; see page 112) for winter cattle food.

from boom to bust

It was all too good to last. By 1900 the Whisky Boom was well and truly over. Why?

- **Too many.** Thirty-three new Scottish distilleries were opened during the 1890s, and many others were expanded.

- **Too much.** Over-production flooded the market (again). In 1889 UK distilleries produced about 19 million gallons (86.4 million litres) of spirit, most of it whisky. By 1900 output had almost doubled, to an astounding 37.1 million gallons (168.7 million litres).

- **Too busy – fighting.** The outbreak of the Boer War between British and Dutch settlers in South Africa in 1899 disrupted the sale of many goods, including whisky.

- **Too risky.** As well as investing in new distilleries, speculators also gambled in whisky-company shares, and even in whisky futures. (Whisky increased in value as it matured, but it was very hard to predict by how much.)

- **Too terrible.** Confidence in whisky as a good-quality, wholesome drink was shattered (for a while) by the Pattison Brothers scandal:

The poor Pattisons

Well, that's how they ended up – and they were sent to gaol. But, for a while, whisky-blending brothers Robert and Walter Pattison of Leith, near Edinburgh,[8] lived a life of fantastic luxury. From humble beginnings, they built up their business (Pattison, Elder and Company) to become one of the market leaders. They lived in fabulous mansions, entertained lavishly, hired private trains, spent a fortune on advertising – and, alas, 'cooked their books'[9] and made fraudulent claims about their whisky. They went bankrupt in 1899, leaving enormous debts behind them – and a nasty taste in the mouths of many of their customers, who discovered that the high-priced and supposedly malt-based, well-matured Pattison blends they had paid for were mostly made of cheap and nasty raw grain whisky.

But while whisky barons in Scotland had been so busy making – and losing – fortunes, whisky distillers elsewhere had not been idle, either…

8. and of talking-parrot fame (see page 135).
9. falsified their accounts.

Moonlight sonata: a Kentucky pioneer at work

CHAPTER EIGHT

MEANWHILE, IN AMERICA...

At first the only spirit distilled in the Colonial New World was the sailors' (and pirates') favourite: rum. Rum was made from imported Caribbean molasses, produced from sugar-cane, grown – alas – by slaves on plantations.[1] The earliest rum distillery that we know about in North America was founded at Boston in 1657, but no doubt there were several earlier, smaller ones. Settlers in the southern colonies also made brandy from whatever fruits they could find – from peaches to pumpkins.

1. Rum was also exported to Africa, and the ships returned laden with African slaves.

Knowledge of how to make whiskey (as the Americans usually spell it) came to Colonial America with Irish, Scottish and Scotch-Irish[2] settlers in the late 17th century. They faced a problem, however. There was very little barley – or malt – in North America. The grain that grew best was corn (maize), so settlers had to find ways of distilling that instead (more about this on pages 151–154).

It was safer to distil the corn than store it and risk it rotting, and more profitable to turn it into whiskey than transport it long distances to markets as raw grain or flour. So settlers sold corn whiskey to towns and cities way back east,[3] or bartered it with local traders for the clothes, tools and farm equipment that they needed.

2. Scots who had moved to live in the north of Ireland during the 17th century. They increased the proportion of Protestants in the region, and supported England's claim to rule Ireland. Many later emigrated to America.

3. Unlike the earliest, rum-drinking settlers, who mostly lived along the eastern seaboard, later 17th-century settlers headed westwards, further inland.

Applejack

There was one fruit spirit that settlers distilled
– at first by accident! In northern colonies,
they left barrels of cider out of doors or in
unheated barns in winter. They found that the
water these contained froze first, leaving
the alcohol in them still liquid. It had been
distilled not by boiling, but by freezing.

Keep out!

At the same time, the North American rum
trade was in trouble. Britain put heavy
customs duties on rum imports from all non-
British colonies, as part of its 17th-century
wars with Spain, the Netherlands and France.
Then British ships blockaded American ports
during the colonists' fight for independence
(1776–1783), so Caribbean ships could not
unload their cargoes. Without molasses, there
could be no rum. Americans began to drink
corn whiskey instead.

'Whiskey' Washington?

'The benefits arising from the moderate use of strong liquor have been experienced in all armies.' So said America's first president, General George Washington (1732–1799). Soldier and statesman Washington was, rather surprisingly, also a distiller. And, around 1775, his Scottish farm manager encouraged him to change from making rum to producing corn whiskey. The venture proved very profitable, but Washington was also the first to tax the newly independent nation of America – by imposing duties on distilled spirits!

In 1783 the USA had won its battle for independence from Britain. But the war had been very expensive, and the new nation began its life with terrible debts. The answer was federal taxation – on all imported goods, as well as on spirits. In fact, the duty levied on whiskey was less than that on rum, but whiskey distillers in the USA (particularly in Pennsylvania) objected very strongly. Therefore, in 1791, the Whisky Rebellion began. Distillers held marches and demonstrations, set fire to effigies of excisemen, or plastered the unfortunate real-life excise officers with tar and feathers.

Such lawlessness could not be tolerated. In 1794 Washington called out the federal troops – for the first time ever, and against the USA's own citizens. This was constitutionally shocking, but it succeeded. Now distillers either paid duties – or (if they didn't and got caught) were severely punished.

We have the technology...

By the early 1800s there were at least 2,000 legal whiskey distillers in the USA – and almost certainly many more illegal ones. But, as we have seen, the whiskey makers were distilling corn, not malted barley. So what, precisely, were they making?

At first, US farm distillers continued to use – or share[4] – small, traditional pot stills, like those used in Ireland or Scotland. If they were

4. Even a simple still was expensive, and early farmers never had much cash. They often bartered their produce, including whiskey, rather than selling it for money. Even finding cash to pay the 1791 Spirit Tax could be a problem.

really poor, they might make do with just a hollowed-out log and a length of old copper piping. But by 1816 at least one company, the Hope Distillery in Louisville, Kentucky, was producing whiskey in giant copper stills on an industrial scale. (It tasted horrible, and was not very popular, but it was a sign of things to come.)

Big or small, the earliest American distillers all began their whiskey-making in a similar way. They simply mashed (ground and soaked) their grain first, then boiled it with water, and either added yeast or allowed wild yeasts to ferment it. But before long, three new developments changed US whiskey for ever:

• **Sweet or sour?**
The 'sour mash' process was invented around 1823 – probably by a Scotsman, Dr James Crow, in Kentucky, but no-one knows for certain. 'Sour mash' sounds rather nasty, but it was simply fermented grain, left over from an earlier batch of whiskey, added to fresh batches of grain and water before they were fermented and distilled.

Why would anyone do this? There were two good reasons. The sour mash was acid, and controlled the growth of 'rogue' bacteria that could spoil the mashed grain as it fermented. It also created ideal conditions in which the yeast could do its work.

• Better burn that barrel!

As more and more settlers reached the USA, the market for whiskey grew larger. Now it was no longer mostly drunk straight from the still by the distiller's family, farmhands and friends. It needed to be packaged for long-distance transport to city shops and country inns, and also carefully stored to mature.[5]

There were millions of trees in America, and American oak was excellent for making barrels to store whiskey in. Some time around 1800 – no-one knows exactly when[6] – it became the custom to 'flame' the insides of barrels before filling them with freshly

5. *Whiskey was traditionally made in autumn, after the grain harvest. But American weather was so harsh, and winter travel conditions were so bad, that farmers had to store the whiskey they had made until the following spring before despatching it.*
6. *It's said that burnt barrels were invented by Kentucky Baptist minister Rev. Elijah Craig, around 1789. He's credited (optimistically) with many other Kentucky 'firsts', from paper-milling to rope-making.*

distilled whiskey. At first this was probably just a way of making sure that they were free from mice and insects, or (if the barrels had been used before, for example, to store salted meat) of cleaning them very thoroughly.

Drinkers soon noticed that the charred particles inside the barrel added colour and flavour to the whiskey – so much so that it was given the nickname 'red liquor'. The charred wood also absorbed sharp, sour, pungent impurities. As a result, the whiskey tasted much better.

• **Flowing through filters**
Not to be outdone by the good citizens of Kentucky, whiskey-makers in the neighbouring state of Tennessee started to filter their whiskey through charcoal made from local sugar-maple trees. They did this straight after the whiskey was distilled, but before it was put into barrels. They claimed it added an extra smoothness and mellowness to the flavour. And they were right, on the whole.

Bourbon (Isn't that a biscuit?)

Barrels also helped name America's best-known whiskey: bourbon. Old Bourbon County became part of the state of Kentucky in 1785. (It was named in honour of the French royal family.) Thanks to its mild climate, fertile farmland and plentiful oakwoods, it became a great place to make good-quality barrel-aged American whiskey. When the barrels were ready to be shipped, dock workers marked them with their place of origin – and the whiskey inside was called the same.

'Bourbon' is often used as another name for all American whiskey. That's not correct – there are several different kinds (see pages 162–163). But confusingly, today's bourbon whiskey no longer has to come from one particular county: it's just a particular style and technique of whiskey-making.

Today, US law states that 'bourbon' may be made anywhere in the USA – although 95% of it does still come from Kentucky. (The rest is made as far away as Colorado, Texas and New

Jersey.) Today there is an annual bourbon festival, and trippers can follow a tourist trail to visit historic Bourbon distilleries.

'Wherever people roamed they needed red liquor to get them along.'[7] And 19th-century Americans did a lot of travelling! Moving on horseback, in covered wagons, or on the newly invented steamships and railways, they crossed the continent, taking whiskey with them – and growing fonder of it.

It's a good job bourbon travels well.

7. *according to Gary Regan and Mardee Haidin Regan,* The Book of Bourbon *(Boston, 1995).*

The new railways – and the telegraph wires strung beside them – also made whiskey sales easier. By 1850, orders could be sent almost instantly, and even the largest consignments could be transported much more quickly than before. Precise figures are impossible, but one historian estimates that between 1850 and 1860, whiskey consumption increased by almost 30% per person.

Stormy weather...

However high, wide and hopeful the prairie skies seemed above whiskey-drinking pioneers and railroad builders, there were clouds looming on the horizon for America's whiskey makers:

• **Civil War!** From 1861 to 1865, northern and southern states fought, chiefly over the issue of slavery. America's whiskey-producing regions were caught in the crossfire. Distilleries were destroyed, cornfields were trampled, business came almost to a standstill. Some whiskey was used, however, by armies on both sides: to numb pain, disinfect wounds – and encourage soldiers.

The cup that cheers

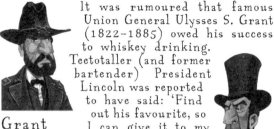

It was rumoured that famous Union General Ulysses S. Grant (1822–1885) owed his success to whiskey drinking. Teetotaller (and former bartender) President Lincoln was reported to have said: 'Find out his favourite, so I can give it to my other generals!'

Grant

But, like many war stories, that may not be true.

Lincoln

• **Scandals!** After the war was over, Grant became US President in 1869 – and was soon involved in scandal. His friends and government colleagues were accused of taking part in the 'Whiskey Ring' – a fraud that took money from whiskey distillers in return for lowering their taxes.

• **Big bad blenders**. After Coffey stills were introduced to the USA, around 1840, vast amounts of cheap alcohol were made from grain, flavoured with all kinds of undesirable additives – from tobacco to nitric acid – then sold as 'blended whiskey'. Traditional pot-still distillers were outraged; they fought a legal battle to define what whiskey was – and was not. The case was only finally settled in 1909 – with a legal compromise about labelling.

• **Price-fixing.** In the 1880s, some of the biggest industrial distilling companies decided to get together to fix the price of whiskey. Nicknamed 'The Whiskey Trust', they were anything but trustworthy. Their aim: to buy up all the small, independent distilleries so that they could control the whole market. They were finally stopped by the federal government, but not until 1895.

• **Taxes, taxes, taxes**. Duty was increased to help pay for the Civil War in 1862; for the rest of the century, distillers campaigned to have it lowered (which it was) or removed (which it wasn't).

• **Hymn-singing ladies**... There had been temperance (anti-drunkenness) campaigners in the USA since 1819. But by the 1870s, anti-alcohol opinions reached a rather alarming high, especially among respectable middle-class women. They gathered in large groups outside bars and liquor stores, praying fervently and singing hymns. In 1874 they founded the Women's Christian Temperance Union (WCTU); it soon became a powerful force in federal politics.

But one female campaigner preferred to continue with direct action...

• **...or an axe-wielding six-footer?** In 1900, tall, well-built Mrs Carrie Nation (1846–1911) hit the headlines after marching into a Kansas drugstore, smashing a liquor-barrel with bricks and setting it on fire. The next year, she attacked a saloon-bar with a hatchet. She was gaoled several times, but as soon as she was freed she reached for her hatchet again. She was expelled from the WCTU – and her husband divorced her.

The formidable Mrs Nation carries out one of her 'hatchetations'

Which whiskey?

By 1900 there was not one, but at least five different kinds of American whiskey to choose from. Can you identify, by sniff or sip, the strong, scented spirit swirling round your glass? Consider this checklist, and see:

• What's it called?

Bourbon? Tennessee? Corn whiskey? Wheat Whiskey? Rye? All these come from the USA.

• What does it taste like?

Light, full, sweet and creamy, like caramel?

Then it's bourbon.

Extra-smooth and very mellow?

Then it's probably from Tennessee.

Young, fresh, light, uncomplicated?

Then it may be corn whiskey. Distilled from at least 81% maize grain, it's often drunk within weeks of leaving the still. Unlike bourbon, it is never left to mature in wooden barrels.

Dry, toasty, nutty, peppery?

That's rye whisky. Originally made by German settlers in Pennsylvania and Maryland from grains brought from home; now made (more confusion!) in Kentucky, and also in Canada. Wheat whisky tastes toasty, too, but also sweet, rich and fruity. And some experts claim to detect hints of peppermint and cherries!

Plain, straightforward, unsurprising?

It's probably blended whisky. Designed to be diluted with cola and soft drinks, or mixed with spirits, fruit and ice in cocktails, blends are made from 20% 'character' whisky plus 80% 'neutral grain spirit'. They may be predictable, but they're cheap – and (maybe) cheering.

• Does it blow your head off?

Traditionally, Tennessee whiskey was sold at higher strength than bourbon: 45% alcohol or more. Or you might have Kentucky whiskey straight from the still – that's an eye-watering 65%–85% alcohol. But relax, it's usually diluted with water to 40% alcohol before it's bottled.

• What does the label say?

By US law, all 'straight' bourbon must be at least 2 years old. If it's under 4 years old, then it must state its age on the label, as well as (like all other whiskeys) its US proof strength and country of origin. Bourbon must also be made from at least 51% corn (maize), have no added colouring or flavouring, be matured in new, charred oak barrels, and be at least 80 US proof.

By the light of the silvery moon

Only *five* American whiskies? Surely there's something we're forgetting? The USA is a very big country, with plenty of places to hide – and plenty of space to make moonshine.

So called (probably by Scots settlers) because it was distilled secretly at night, by the light of the moon, 'moonshine' is home-made, illegal, non-duty-paid whisky. It was – and still is – produced in simple pot stills, from any grain, fruit or root that can be mixed with water and fermented.

Moonshine's strength and quality varies from one individual distiller to another. But its alternative names – 'white lightning' and 'mountain dew' – tell us quite a lot about it.

• **Appearance:** Clear, like water. This means that it's drunk fresh, and not stored or matured in barrels.

• **Place of manufacture:** Wild, remote areas, such as mountains.

• **Powerful – and sometimes lethal – effect on drinkers:** If carefully made, and diluted with water, moonshine is, in theory, no less safe to drink than other alcohols. But if badly made, it can be contaminated either by poisonous alcohols in feints and foreshots (see pages 113 and 114), or by toxins, such as lead solder, in distilling equipment and containers.

You have been warned!

Another Scottish stereotype?

In 1964, US law decreed that whiskey storage barrels, burnt or not, could only be used once. So canny, thrifty Scottish distillers bought up all the empties from America – and also thousands of used sherry barrels from Spain. They used these to store their own Scotch malt and blended whiskies, claiming that each different type of barrel added its own 'special something' to the final product.

Today, the American oak flavour has become so important that one big distilling company has purchased its own forest in Kentucky, to ensure a future supply of American white oak for its barrels.

Second best?

For all its faults, moonshine has had many admirers:

> 'Well, between Scotch and nothin', I suppose I'd take Scotch. It's the nearest thing to good moonshine I can find.'
>
> *American novelist William Faulkner (1897–1962)*

And, by the time that Faulkner was writing, Scotch whisky was admired worldwide…

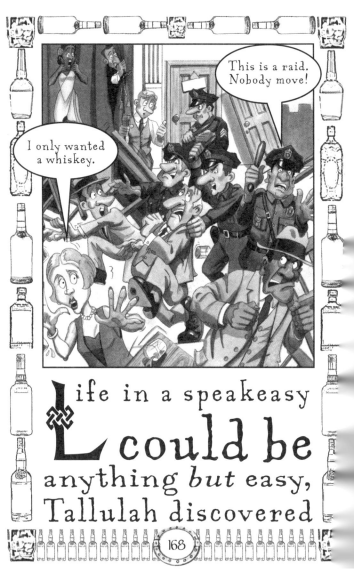

CHAPTER NINE

WHISKY GOES GLOBAL

Back in Scotland and the rest of the British Isles, the whisky industry took a long time to recover from the 1890s crash (see page 144). Slowly, sales and profits increased, but there were setbacks:

• **A 'Welsh wizard' who didn't like whisky**
That was what they called British finance minister David Lloyd George (1863–1945). He famously said that 'Alcohol is more damaging than German submarines.' Between 1909 and 1914 he raised the duty on sprits by around 30% – and UK alcohol consumption fell by the same amount.

• **More 'whisky wars'** – this time, a three-sided tussle between the whisky industry and brewers (who owned the pubs and wanted their customers to drink beer, not spirits), and between malt-whisky and grain-whisky distillers.

• **Warplanes and weak whisky**

The outbreak of World War I in 1914 hit whisky producers still further. Although big grain distilling companies made money selling non-drinkable products – surgical spirit as antiseptic, yeast for baking bread, and 'dope' (a protective coating) for aircraft – whisky profits fell sharply. Duties on alcohol were increased several times, as the government badly needed money. And, in a bid to end drunkenness among the troops, the alcoholic strength of spirits was reduced, and pub opening hours were strictly limited.

Millie, I hope that dope isn't making you light-headed.

What is whisky?

In 1905, London magistrates prosecuted pub landlords for selling a drink that was 'not of the nature, substance or quality demanded by the purchaser'. It was, in fact, raw grain spirit with just a few drops of cheap whisky added for flavour. To add insult to injury, some of it was mockingly labelled 'NSS' – 'Never Seen Scotland'! The court found the landlords guilty, and declared that 'real' whisky could only be made in a traditional pot still, using malted barley.

The big grain distillers and their customers, the blenders, were horrified. They appealed the court's decision, and in 1909 they won their case. The legal definition of whisky pronounced by the court was to last for exactly 100 years: Whisky could be made from any kind of grain, in any kind of still, but whisky labelled 'Scotch' had to be distilled in Scotland.

In 2009, new laws gave the name – and the product – 'Scotch whisky' much more precise protection. Today, Scotch whisky can only be described in one of these five ways: • **single malt** • **single grain** • **blended malt** • **blended grain** • **blended Scotch whisky.** Vague, misleading terms such as 'pure malt' are not allowed. Most important of all, any whisky sold as 'Scotch' must be wholly distilled and matured in Scotland. Single-malt whiskies must be bottled in Scotland, too. Distillery names can only be used for whisky made on the premises.

Prohibition!

Surprisingly, the end of the 'war to end all wars' in 1918 did not end government restrictions on alcohol – or temperance campaigners' bids to ban it. In Russia, the revolutionary new Communist regime continued the Tsars' wartime prohibition of alcohol. Even Scotland held a national temperance referendum (in 1920 – the prohibitionists lost). And, across the Atlantic, anti-alcohol campaigners won their fight to ban the manufacture, sale and supply of all alcoholic beverages.

American 'Prohibition' lasted from 1920 until 1933. It looked like a fatal blow for Scottish whisky producers. But it wasn't. Why?

• Although alcohol consumption in the USA did fall, demand did not go away. People still wanted whisky! And when they dressed up for a night on the town and sashayed out to a speakeasy,[1] what they were offered was very often Scotch. Since US whiskey distilling was

1. *A bar selling illegal alcohol; entry was by speaking a secret password, hence 'speakeasy'.*

banned, the only available strong alcohol was either local moonshine or a branded, bottled blend from overseas.

• Wise drinkers paid a little more for the tried and tested Scotch. They did not want to risk going blind, or – like over 12,000 moonshine drinkers during Prohibition – ending up dead.

Prohibition: government agents destroy alcohol stocks

But it's medicinal!

Some Scotch whisky sellers came up with a clever – and legal – way to circumvent US Prohibition. They declared that Scotch whisky – especially smoky, peaty malt whisky – had 'medicinal virtues', and arranged for it to be sold, in single doses, by American chemists. Medicinal whisky was hardly glamorous, seductive or convivial. On the other hand, whisky cocktails were all three:

Cheers!

So, travel back in time. Relax and chill… There's jazz playing – the latest, wildest sounds. There are pretty girls – with cropped hair! in short skirts! (daring new fashions) – dancing the Charleston (so clever, but outrageous!). There are handsome male crooners, a famous writer gathering material for his next detective best-seller, a film star or two, and smartly dressed gamblers (also illegal) huddled around card-tables. There are rich and poor and black and white all enjoying a good time together (most other places in twenties America are racially segregated). A wisecracking barman is mixing cocktails, and a not-so-dumb-blonde waitress is serving them:

- **Manhattan:** whisky + sweet vermouth + ice

- **Old-Fashioned:** sugar + bitters[2] + whisky + ice + lemon peel

- **Barbary Coast:** whisky + gin + chocolate liqueur + ice + cream (ugh!)

Don't try these at home unless you are over 18 – and even then, drink responsibly. These are extremely powerful!

2. bitters: herbs and spices steeped in alcohol, originally sold as a remedy for stomach ailments.

Cocktails?

Yes, it's a strange name to give to a drink – and no, no-one knows how it happened. The world's first-known cocktail party was held in 1917, in Missouri, USA. Soon, cocktails were very fashionable. At first, a cocktail contained simply spirit, ice, bitters and perhaps sugar and water. Later the name was given to any mixed drink based on spirits.

Walk on the wild side

But – don't look now! – who's that just walked in? Expensive suit, snakelike smile, a very shady lady – and six psychopathic bodyguards. Yes sir! It's the local 'Mr Big'. Bootlegging[3] gangsters like him supply the whisky that you're drinking. It's shipped to islands, such as the Bahamas, outside US government control, then ferried northwards towards US ports. High-powered launches meet the ships while they're still in international waters, offload their whisky, and bring it ashore. More whisky comes from Scotland via Canada, and from the Caribbean. They say that Al Capone, America's most notorious gangster, makes $60 million a year from smuggling drink – though he has to bribe police and excise officials, of course.

3. bootlegging: smuggling; the name came from hiding containers of alcohol in the boots or trousers.

Survival strategies

Heavy taxes, war, Prohibition, a worldwide economic slump in the 1930s, and then war again from 1939 to 1945. How could the whisky industry survive?

• **By buying up and shutting down.** These tactics by big grain distillers closed many of Scotland's – and Ireland's – small, traditional distilleries. By the mid-1930s only about 15 survived in Scotland, compared with over 150 in 1900.

• **By spreading the word.** The 1930s saw some of the world's first moving-picture advertisements, in the cinema and 'bright light' city-centre displays, together with stylish magazine and poster images.

• **By battling on for Britain.** Making whisky in wartime was not easy. Taxes were raised yet again. Ships carrying grain – and whisky – were sunk. To save grain for baking bread, whisky-making was stopped altogether in 1943, and it remained rationed until 1953.

Whisky Galore

In 1941 the cargo ship SS *Politician* was wrecked off the Scottish island of Eriskay while carrying around 240,000 bottles of whisky. Many of these were 'helped' ashore by islanders, and hidden. So were rolls of banknotes, destined for South America. The wreck was eventually blown up by the authorities to discourage further salvaging.

A safe and sanitised version of the shipwreck story became the basis of the 1947 novel *Whisky Galore* by Scottish author Sir Compton Mackenzie. In 1949 it was made into a film, crammed full of caricature 'stage Scots'.

In 2008, divers searched the wreck and recovered some more bottles. One was sold at auction for £2,200.

Dynamiting whisky – you wouldn't think there'd be men in the world so crazy as that!

Angus John Campbell, former boatswain of the Politician

Export – or die!

In 1945, war-torn Britain had no money; the only hope for whisky makers was to sell their products overseas. By the late 1950s, over a third of the UK's total whisky production was exported, mostly to the USA. Sales to Europe also increased after the UK joined the EEC[4] in 1973. By the late 1970s, over 100 million bottles of whisky left Britain every year. And cheap mass tourism created a new market for 'duty-free'.

But not everything in the Highland glens – or on the whisky factory floors – was perfect. Almost all the UK exports were blends, and so was most of the whisky drunk outside Scotland. No-one, except the Scots, wanted malt whisky.

A further problem loomed. By the 1980s the US market was saturated. Everyone who liked whisky was already buying it – and they were getting older. Young Americans, and even young Scots, saw blended whisky –

4. *The European Economic Community (often called the Common Market), the predecessor of the EU (European Union).*

marketed with slogans such as 'Born 1820 and still going strong' – as an old-fashioned drink. They wanted something new, and mostly they chose cheap, mass-produced, skilfully marketed vodka.[5]

Was traditional 'pure' malt whisky now old history? Were blends boring and fuddy-duddy? Was Scotch whisky dead? Many might have said so. But in the later 1960s, whisky marketeers – led by the Glenfiddich malt-whisky distillery (founded 1887) – had one very bright idea indeed.

They would create a new, exclusive, luxury market for Scotland's 'rare' and 'precious' malts. Tastefully packaged, expensively priced, and surrounded by enough 'misty mountain' copy to sell a million Highland holidays – plus countless facts and baffling jargon to please whisky connoisseurs and distillery geeks – they'd become a status symbol for the fortunate few. Sipping them would be a privilege. You'd be drinking Scotland's heritage.

5. Ironically, a lot of vodka was made in Scotland as well, but this did not really help the whisky industry.

Whisky wonderland

The rest, as they say, is history. And this time it's true. Glenfiddich – it also had an instantly recognisable triangular bottle – became the world's best-selling malt whisky, and remains so today. Other distillers soon joined the new malt-whisky bonanza. Even if consumers could not afford a whole bottle of 'single malt' whisky, they wanted to taste it in their favourite blends. Much malt-whisky-inspired fun soon followed: whisky fairs, whisky festivals, whisky tastings and whisky tourism.

In 2009, one in twelve of all visitors to Scotland toured a distillery – an amazing 1,268,553 men, women and children. They sniffed the malt, puzzled at the pipework, admired the gleaming stills, sipped (if old enough) the finished product, bought the pretty tea towel or souvenir bottle(s), and listened to charming stories about Scottish ghosts, Scottish heroes – and distillery cats.[6] In the same year, whisky exports reached a

6. *Towser, who lived at Glenturret distillery, was reckoned to have caught an astounding 28,899 mice in her 24-year career. This figure was based on an officially observed sample period, during which Towser caught an average of 3 mice per day.*

staggering £3.1 billion, generating – as whisky producers proudly proclaimed – £90 every second for the UK economy.

All round the world, whisky experts wrote books and set up websites, comparing and sharing tasting notes. Whisky collectors spent vast fortunes chasing down elusive bottles. In 2009, the world's largest whisky collection – 3,384 bottles amassed over 35 years by Brazilian businessman Claive Vidiz – was purchased and returned 'home' to Scotland. At the same time, bottles containing £2.2 billion of blended whisky and £454 million of malt whisky were shipped from Scotland overseas.

Whisky has also reached new and different frontiers: in 2008 it powered a sports car on Islay (0–60 in 3.5 seconds!), purified water in northeast Scotland and (as draff) pioneered bio-energy generation from waste. And at Christmas 2009, undecided gift-givers could download the world's first 'Malt-Matcher' iPhone app, to help them choose the best bottle for each friend.

Going global

Well done, Scotland! However, all through the 20th century, big Scottish distillers had bought up weaker ones. And increasingly, from the 1960s, Scottish distillers, big and small, had joined with, or been taken over by, larger international conglomerates. Many are based outside Scotland, and some outside the UK. This has had some unfortunate consequences.

End of an era

In 2009, there were mass protests when a multinational drinks company closed down the ancient and iconic Johnnie Walker bottling plant at Kilmarnock in Lowland Scotland. The business had been running since 1820, when John Walker first sold whisky from a licensed grocer's shop. About 700 jobs were feared lost.

In 2009, 40% of all Scotland's distilleries were foreign-owned. Just four companies controlled 62% of the Scottish malt-whisky industry and 85% of the Scottish grain-whisky industry. The largest, Diageo, was based in London, England; the second-largest, Pernod Ricard, was based in Paris, France.

A world of whiskies

Most surprising of all, the last years of the 20th century and the start of the new millennium have seen the birth of new whisky-making industries all round the world.

Switzerland
Netherlands   Liechtenstein
Belgium   Germany
France   Austria   Sweden
Finland
Canada
Scotland
USA
Ireland
Wales
England   Japan
Spain   Taiwan
India
Brazil
Argentina   South Africa   Australia
New Zealand

Whisky-producing countries
2011

Drinkers of world whiskies can look forward to many delights and surprises – not least among the many new brand names. From Switzerland's accurate (though confusing) 'Swiss Highlander' and Japan's 'Super Nikka', via the predictable New Zealand 'Kiwi' and Welsh 'Rugby Union', to the puzzling Swedish 'Smoky Duck', new-age Indian 'Amrut Fusion', or frankly alarming German 'Blue Mouse' (how many glasses have *you* had?), each different brand, or blend, has something special to offer.

'Scotch' may no longer be Scottish-owned – but whisky is now worldwide!

Slàinte!

Timeline of distilleries in the British Isles

still active in 2010

- **Speyside malt**
1786 Strathisla
1810/1829 Glenburgie
1810/1836 Glenfarclas
1821 Linkwood
1823/4 Balmenach
1823/4 Mortlach
1824 Cardhu
1824 Glenlivet
1824 Macallan
1824 Miltonduff
1826 Aberlour
1826 Glendronach
1835 Benrinnes
1840 Glen Grant
1852 Dailuaine
1869 Cragganmore
1871 Inchgower
1876 Glenlossie
1878 Glen Rothes
1878/1880 Glen Spey
1887 Glenfiddich
1891 Craigellachie
1891 Strathmill
1892 Balvenie
1894 Longmorn
1895 Dufftown
1895/6 Aultmore
1897 Glendullan
1897 Glen Moray
1897 Speyburn
1897 Tamdhu
1897 Tomatin

1898 Ardmore
1898 Benriach
1898 Benromach
1898 Glentauchers
1898 Glen Elgin
1898 Knockando
1899 Dallas Dhu – now a
   working museum
1958 Tormore
1962 Macduff
1964 Tomintoul
1967 Glenallachie
1971 Mannochmore
1973 Braeval – Scotland's
   highest distillery
1975 Allt-a-Bhainne
1990 Kininvie
1990 Speyside
2010 Roseisle

- **Highland malt**
1775 Glenturret
1785 Glen Garioch
1790 Balblair
1794 Oban
1798 Blair Athol
1812 Royal Brackla
1817 Teaninich
1819 Brora/Clynelish
1824 Fettercairn
1825 Ben Nevis
1825 Edradour –
   Scotland's smallest

1825 Glencadam
1826 Old Pultney
1826 Royal Lochnagar
1833 Glengoyne
1838 Glen Ord
1839 Dalmore
1843 Glenmorangie
1894 An Cnoc/ Knockdhu
1895 Drumguish
1896 Aberfeldy
1897 Dalwhinnie
1949 Tullibardine
1957 Lochside
1965 Deanston
1974 Auchroisk

• Highland grain
1961 Invergordon

• Lowland malt
1772 Littlemill – possibly
  Scotland's oldest
1800/1826 Auchentoshan
1817 Bladnoch
1837 Glenkinchie
1965/6 Loch Lomond

• Lowland grain
1811 Port Dundas –
  scheduled to close 2010
1824 Cameron Bridge
1885 North British
1927 Strathclyde
1936 Girvan
1994 Loch Lomond

• Islay and Islands malt
1779 Bowmore – waste
  water heats a swimming
  pool

1794 Ardbeg
1798 Tobermory
1810 Isle of Jura
1815 Laphroaig
1816 Lagavulin – first
  owner drowned in one
  of its wash tubs
1830 Talisker (Skye)
1846 Caol Ila
1880 Bunnahabhain
1881 Bruichladdich
1995 Isle of Arran

• Campbeltown malt
1828 Springbank
1832 Glen Scotia – said to
  be haunted!

• Orkney malt
1790/1798 Highland Park
  – Scotland's most
  northerly distillery
1885 Scapa

• Ireland
1608 Bushmills,
  Co. Antrim – oldest by far
1757 Locke's,
  Co. Westmeath*
1780 (or before)
  Jameston, Dublin*
1820 Middleton, Co. Cork
1987 Cooley, Co. Louth

• England
2006 St George's

• Wales
2000 Penderyn

  * *Working whiskey museums.*

Index

www.salariya.com
where books come to life!

Follow us on Facebook and Twitter

Children's non-fiction and graphic novels

The Book House blog competitions, giveaways and current news

Fiction for children and teenagers

www.youtube.com/user/BookHo

Download our free iPhone and iPad catalogue app. Go to http://bit.ly/c8zQuy or search for Salariya or Book House at the App Store

Four free web books